# THE MORALE OF THE AMERICAN REVOLUTIONARY ARMY

# *The Morale of the American Revolutionary Army*

By Allen Bowman
Introduction by Arthur Pope

KENNIKAT PRESS, INC./PORT WASHINGTON, N. Y.

THE MORALE OF THE AMERICAN REVOLUTIONARY ARMY


This Edition published in 1964 by Kennikat Press, Inc by arrangement with the copyright holder.

Manufactured in the United States of America

Library of Congress Catalog Card No: 64-25652

# *Introduction*

Despite extraordinary development in equipment, the basic factors of war remain curiously constant. Perhaps the most universal and important of these factors is morale. Although it is now studied and talked about far more than ever before, it stands for a reality that has decided most wars in the past. Every great general has highly prized and exploited morale to the utmost. Alexander, Hannibal, Cromwell, and Napoleon understood how to evoke from their armies power, bravery, achievement that seemed beyond normal capacity. They knew how to steady their troops, how to keep them compact and durable in the face of adverse circumstances.

Yet there are always new names for old verities and new ways of exploiting them. Each war has its own slogans and its own presumed discoveries. It would seem that it was in the course of World War I that propaganda emerged as a "new" weapon. The intensive German studies undertaken at the close of that war emphasized British propaganda as the most deadly of the Allied weapons. They revealed that the German public's will to endure and conquer was insufficient and that internal psychological collapse ultimately involved military surrender.

It is the effect of propaganda on the morale of man—on his will to work, to fight, and to endure—that spells military defeat or success. The rediscovery of this ancient truth has led recently to a more conscious recognition of morale, to a more exact appraisal of its major role in wartime. Since the close of World War I, the widespread effort to understand and utilize morale has been manifest in about 5,000 studies on various aspects of the subject. The progress of psychology and the social sciences (including special disciplines like cultural anthropology) has offered prospects for the control of morale never before envisaged.

The Germans have lavished immense resources of men and funds on the problems of morale. A survey of the Committee for National Morale, *Axis Grand Strategy*, summarizes many of their outstanding strategical and tactical policies and shows that at every point morale has been a major consideration. The Germans have developed an extraordinarily effective psychological offensive which has done much to disintegrate the countries they have victimized. They have explored every avenue of domestic and foreign terrorization, every technique for fortifying the will of their own nation, every means of inspiring confusion and division among potential enemies.

The Russians have built up morale with sound and adroit educational methods, exploiting the native love of country to the full and organizing miscellaneous types of morale service, from the political commissars (who are really morale officers partaking in fighting) in the armed forces, down through every element of industry and civilian life.

Although the United States has recognized the importance of the problem, its national policy in this connection has been fragmented into so many separate elements and functions that our war effort has by no means had the full advantage of available knowledge. As the Committee for National Morale has insisted from the start, morale is as indivisible as security. It is global and organic and its component elements and consequences may support or cancel one another. Its consistent and comprehensive exploitation requires a pooling of scientific resources by agencies and persons able to look over compartmental walls and to develop loyal team work.

There is now a steadily accumulating body of knowledge about morale which should be concerted into a comprehensive and practical guide to methods of dealing with separate problems and of guaranteeing their consistent treatment. Certain problems of morale necessitate experimental investigation; ascertained principles in psychological fields are applicable to many morale problems. But these problems are so vast and so complicated that no adequate solution is possible until all relevant types of data have been coordinated and exploited.

One of the most productive fields of research is, of course, history. In the panorama of yesterday we can see morale operating on a huge scale in terms of principles deeply grounded in human nature and social action, principles that have a considerable degree of universal validity. Hence, the importance of historical studies of morale, of which Prof. Bowman's book is an excellent example. The American Revolutionary War provides one of the most instructive morale situations that history offers and one that has long called for exposition. It is not enough to say that Washington had great tenacity, that courage and endurance persevered at Valley Forge, that, despite harrowing conditions, sheer force of will wrought victory. Such generalizations are of limited value. What has been needed is a factual, objective, and thoroughly documented study. This Prof. Bowman has accomplished in a systematic and workmanlike fashion.

The present study, unprecedentedly complete, throws a new light on the whole morale situation of the Revolutionary War. Prof. Bowman's account reveals the startling morale heterogeneity in the Revolutionary forces.

There were many men of incredible courage and endurance, men who stood up without flinching, day after day, to a cruel ordeal; men who stood firm despite exceedingly trying circumstances. Here character and faith were clearly exhibited as the greatest forces in sustaining morale. But the indolent, the timid, the selfish, the dishonest, the extreme individualists, and the faint-hearted gave way, under pressure, to panic, despair, even treason.

The colonies were by no means well organized or controlled by the common standards and traditions which in more advanced societies tend to conceal some of the primitive aspects of morale. The indolence and frequent indifference of the Continental Congress, the only inclusive governing body, had a paralyzing effect on the Revolutionary forces. Moreover, civilian support in sharing common dangers, sacrifice, and loyalty were frequently lacking.

Some of the morale problems identifiable in conditions in 1776 offer revealing similarities to present situations. The military inexperience of both the army and the civilian populations in assigning false values to military objectives offers some salutary lessons and the effect of the prestige of the handsomely clothed, beautifully maneuvering British soldiers has its counterpart in today's myth of German invincibility.

The importance of taking into account habits and traditions in directing war adjustments is also pointedly revealed in various aspects of the Revolutionary War. We are reminded that even a great ideal frequently cannot bridge the dangerous cleft when individual habits and preferences run directly counter to the severe demands of discipline—a problem that we have not yet wholly solved. Among the other elements of significance, historically and for our own time, were the importance of dependable supplies, food and clothing, regularity of furloughs, terms of enlistment, and other basic uniformities in structure and organization. The problems involved put a dangerous and demoralizing strain on the entire Revolutionary effort.

Reference should of course be made to the positive side of Revolutionary experience in the morale field. Chaplains were useful; had there been more of them, there would have been fewer morale difficulties. Music was early seen to be an advantage. Washington magnificently exemplified inspiring leadership based on character and devotion. Above all, the factor that seems to have been most effective—although it did not by any means inspire all—was confidence in the rightness of the Revolutionary cause and great faith that it would triumph.

Many of the factors of morale are still too little understood and until they have been more thoroughly explored they cannot be properly controlled. Further studies of the whole question are needed, particularly historical accounts of this type, which amplify as well as provide checks for the experimental and theoretical work on the subject.

The Committee for National Morale is happy to endorse Professor Bowman's study. It is hoped that other scholars will turn their talents to this most promising and important field.

ARTHUR UPHAM POPE

*Chairman,*
*Committee for National Morale*

# *Preface*

The present work is the result of research begun many years ago under the late Professor C. H. Van Tyne, and it owes much to his inspiration. The project was continued under the supervision of present members of the Department of History at the University of Michigan, particularly Professors Verner Winslow Crane and A. E. R. Boak. Their constant attention and constructive criticism are greatly appreciated. The thoughtfulness of Dr. Howard Peckham and of others at the William L. Clements Library has been exceedingly helpful, not to speak of the courtesy shown me in the Library of Congress, the Boston Public Library, the National Archives, and in numerous historical society libraries in New England.

I wish also to express appreciation for the interest which the American Council on Public Affairs has shown in this work for a considerable time—an interest which has made possible this presentation of the results to the general public.

The illustration on the title page appears through the courtesy of the Bettmann Archive.

ALLEN BOWMAN

*Professor of History,*
*Marion College, Indiana*

# Contents

# ☆ I ☆

# *Physical Factors*

## THE QUALITY OF TROOPS

Many of the men who assembled about Boston when the Revolution broke out were proved soldiers, experienced in the French and Indian War.[1] From the first, George Washington was more concerned about the proper selection of officers than about the general quality of the rank and file.[2] Many substantial New England farmers enlisted early in the war.[3] Muster rolls of Connecticut, New York, and Pennsylvania regiments show a considerable proportion of married men, farmers, and skilled workmen.[4] Washington formed a high opinion of the veterans who remained with him through years of hardship.[5]

On the other hand, there is much evidence that the army included some decidedly inferior elements. After the initial outburst of enthusiasm in 1775 had subsided, recruiting became more difficult every year.[6] In 1776 some 89,600 men enlisted, but by 1781 the number of recruits had dwindled to 29,340.[7] The original decision of Congress to pay no bounties (November 30, 1775) gave way in less than ten months to an offer of $20 and 100 to 200 acres of land.[8] The States quickly resorted to the draft.[9] Congressional and State bounties rose steadily, until in 1780 Washington received recruits who had been given $150 in specie for five months' service. Before the end of the war the worried Commander-in-Chief actually recommended enrolling Hessian prisoners.[10]

Obviously under such conditions recruiting officers were tempted to accept unfit men. Recruiting standards were none too high. Tricky officers, relying heavily on the stimulus of drink, brought ignorant and unreliable men into the service.[11] Continental soldiers who enlisted as substitutes for exempted militiamen were often unfit.[12] In one way and another large numbers of mere boys and infirm old men appeared in the ranks.[13] Officers characterized some of their troops as "sweepings of the York streets," "Food for Worms—miserable sharp looking Caitiffs, hungry lean fac'd Villains," and deplored the lack of military academies for making real soldiers.[14] Physical unfitness constituted a major problem. Despite Washington's efforts to maintain high standards, a return of the New England men in 1781 showed almost a tenth of the recruits so evidently unfit that they had to be sent home after they reached the army.[15] Militia drafts throughout the war produced a host of undesirables.[16] Nathanael Greene characterized the troops he obtained from the militia of the Carolinas as "the worst in the world" and "of no more use than if they were in the moon." He actually questioned whether the few militia who adhered to Francis Marion and Thomas Sumter were not more interested in plunder than in the Revolutionary cause.[17]

Very serious for army morale was the presence of many men of foreign birth. One of Washington's earliest orders forbade the use of foreigners as sentries unless they had families in America to whom they were known to be attached.[18] Natives of the British Isles were especially under suspicion.[19] Washington insisted that his private guard be not only men of property but also of American birth and that Stephen Moylan's light horse contingent, consisting largely of foreigners, be debarred from important duties such as reconnoitering.[20] By the summer of 1777 desertion among foreign-born soldiers had become so general that Washington warned against enlisting more, especially for the cavalry (whose equipment was expensive), unless the candidates were obviously of good character and well recommended.[21] In the following year he told Count Pulaski that the cavalry must without exception be natives.[22] Joseph Galloway declared that three-fourths of the deserters who came into Philadelphia from Valley Forge were foreigners.[23] To what extent the foreign element in the Pennsylvania and New Jersey lines was a cause of the mutiny of 1781 is problematical.[24] But it is significant that the roll of the 11th Pennsylvania Regiment in 1779 shows foreigners outnumbering natives two to one, with the Irish alone comprising nearly half of the men whose birthplaces are recorded.[25] The roster of the Pennsylvania State Regiment of Artillery shows that the majority of that unit were born in the British Isles and Germany, the Irish again forming the largest single element—comprising about a third of the entire regiment.[26] It is also significant that the German regiment caused most trouble after the mutiny.[27] It is evident that the large foreign element seriously complicated the problem of morale.

Still more troublesome was the enlistment of convicts, Loyalists, prisoners of war, and deserters from the enemy. In May, 1777, Washington protested to Congress and Gov. Patrick Henry of Virginia against the buying of convict servants by recruiting officers. Such recruits, he declared, were absolutely unreliable and likely to desert at any time. Some of them were "Foreigners of no principle."[28] Nathanael Greene was likewise distrustful of the Virginia convicts who were serving with him in Pennsylvania early in 1778.[29] The southern States lightheartedly relieved themselves of criminals by compelling them to serve time as Continental soldiers.[30] Militiamen who deserted or proved to be otherwise delinquent were disposed of in like manner.[31] Greene actually approved of Continental enlistment of the runaways from the battle of Guilford Court House.[32] Loyalists were sometimes pardoned by the States on condition that they join the patriot army.[33] Drafts in disaffected districts were likely to net officers and men who were Tories at heart.[34] As early as October 11, 1776, Washington complained that the service had already suffered greatly from Tory desertion, and forbade receiving "persons of Disaffected and Suspicious Character."[35] But, as his own orderly book shows, it was impossible to keep them out.[36] All but 130 of the prisoners taken at King's Mountain were paroled and enlisted in the militia service for three months—a piece of folly that merely lost the patriots some 600 prisoners for exchange.[37] By various methods, including offers of pardon and the drafting of non-jurors, the South sent in Loyalists until the end of the war, although Greene confessed that such troops were inferior.[38] Indeed, to use his own words, North Carolina furnished him "few other Soldiers than non jurors and disaffected."[39]

Congress early disapproved of using prisoners of war. In 1776 it ordered the discharge of those already enlisted,[40] but this was little heeded. Similar action, broadened to include enemy deserters, was necessary two years later because of the mischief that had resulted from such heedlessness.[41] Similarly futile was a further recommendation that prisoners and deserters from the British service be excluded from the militia. Massachusetts and New York, to be sure, soon enacted legislation, but New York named only the foreign-born; Pennsylvania acted only after two years' delay; the Carolinas took no interest until the war was practically over, and left large loopholes in their legislation.[42] Such laws were apparently poorly enforced. Washington spoke repeatedly for six years against the use of deserters and prisoners.[43] But he recognized exceptions in the case of Pulaski's and Armand's independent corps and the German volunteers—exceptions which lowered the general standard and involved both civil and military authorities in no end of trouble. Fully half of Pulaski's corps in 1778 consisted of deserters and prisoners.[44] The treachery of Armand's corps in that same year gave a pointed illustration of what might be expected of such troops.[45]

While there is no way of estimating the number of undesirables in the army as a whole, it is evident that the total was large enough to produce a serious lowering of morale.

### SUPPLIES

The best supplied armies, what with the monotony of camp life and the stress of active service, have always presented problems of shifting morale. Needless to say, such problems are far more difficult when men are poorly armed, ill clad, hungry, and inadequately paid. Revolutionary army morale was constantly affected by such privations.

Munitions of war were never adequate. Scarcity of powder and of cartridge paper compelled the patriot troops to carry fewer rounds of ammunition than did British regulars during most of the war.[1] Guns, bayonets, tools, and other equipment were woefully inadequate.[2] Only French aid made continued resistance possible.[3] There were times during the years 1779-1781 when lack of munitions alone made it impossible for Washington to undertake extensive operations.[4] Southern leaders were still more hampered than those in the North by lack of materials of all kinds. No tents, horses, or wagons; no firearms or artillery; no cartridge boxes or canteens or paper—such are the constant complaints of officers in Virginia, the Carolinas, and Georgia.[5] Henry Lee asserted that "no general ever commanded troops worse appointed or worse supplied."[6]

Still more serious was the lack of food and clothing. When men were cold and hungry, their discontent reached the danger point.[7] There were serious complaints as to quality of rations in the early months of the war.[8] By 1777 dissatisfaction in Washington's army became general. In May an acute shortage of food compelled the Commander-in-Chief to appeal to the Commissary General for action to keep the army from dispersing.[9] This plea is typical of many that generals were forced to make during the entire war. In spite of the abundance of food in the country, Washington's men for months scarcely tasted vegetables and had little salt or vinegar, while the liquor supply—always considered essential in those days—was totally inadequate.[10] At Valley Forge (1777-1778) the troops were brought literally to the verge of starvation. Only with the greatest difficulty was the army kept from open mutiny.[11] At Morristown during the extremely severe winter of 1779-1780 the suffering was almost if not quite as acute.[12] At practically all times Washington's army lived from hand to mouth.[13]

In North, South, and West the food supply was still more precarious during most of the war than in the Middle Department where Washington was in immediate command. The posts farthest north often suffered extremely.[14] Benedict Arnold's march to Quebec was marked by ghastly scenes of starvation.[15] Lack of food for the militia in frontier districts almost destroyed the value of such troops.[16] Western posts were so miserably supplied that mutiny was often imminent.[17] In Virginia Lafayette found his men deserting for want of flour and rum. The farmers, like those of Pennsylvania in 1777-1778, demanded specie for their produce. An army might as well have marched through a desert instead of a land flowing with milk and honey.[18] Troops in the Carolinas suffered incredible hardships.[19] Greene's half-starved men sometimes fainted on the march.[20] After Yorktown the South simply forgot its army, leaving the troops to seize corn meal from the markets by unashamed force.[21] Anthony Wayne had to forage for his men in Georgia as best he could.[22] The food supply, in short, was so precarious everywhere throughout the war that army morale was constantly menaced.

Lack of clothing, blankets, and tents added greatly to the distress. As early as the fall of 1776, nakedness began to demoralize Washington's troops.[23] It was no small factor in the extensive desertion of such periods as the winter of 1777-1778.[24] At one time upward of two thirds of his force were practically barefoot.[25] Thousands of men went without blankets, and many were rendered unfit for duty. "Our sick naked, our well naked, our unfortunate men in captivity naked!" cried the Commander-in-Chief in anguish of spirit.[26] Much sickness, desertion, and death could have been prevented by adequate clothing.[27] "Cold and nakedness," complained the Virginia officers to their State Assembly in 1781, "have swept off four fold more of your troops, than all the malice of a cruel enemy has ever been able to destroy."[28]

Soldiers in the North as well as those at Valley Forge could be tracked through the snow by the blood from freezing, lacerated feet.[29] Many blankets were only two-thirds large enough.[30] Only too often the distribution of the few supplies at hand was very unequal, even in the same army, and detached corps were neglected.[31] Wayne had to divide clothing for 600 men among thirteen regiments early in 1778 to prevent a mutiny.[32] In March he had to wait for shoes before he could march from Haddonfield.[33]

Depressing as the situation was in Middle and Northern Departments, it was even worse in the South. Virginia seemed paralyzed during most of the war as far as supplying her troops was concerned.[34] Horatio Gates and Greene waited in vain for reinforcements from that State because the men were too naked to march.[35] It is impossible to present here all the harrowing details concerning the plight of the troops in the Carolinas. Performing extremely hard duty, the men there should have had several outfits of clothing in a year, but in reality received almost none from the public.[36] Greene's march from Guilford Court House to the Dan River was marked by bloody tracks.[37] A return of clothing in one brigade at the High Hills of Santee in August, 1781, showed 367 men fit for duty possessing 37 coats, of which 34 needed repair, 53 vests, 32 of them in need of repair, 143 good pairs of shoes, and 198 blankets. Shirts were just sufficient to go around, with none for changing, and linen overalls were only a little more numerous.[38] At one time nearly half of Greene's force lacked shoes, and there was not one blanket for each ten men.[39] In later months it was not unusual for half his little army to be unfit for duty because of nakedness.[40]

### SICKNESS

The extraordinary sufferings just described—together with the more usual hardships of war, mismanagement, and the primitive state of medical knowledge—produced much sickness. Long marches by ill-clad, undernourished men in inclement weather, use of impure drinking water, occasional lack of wood for heating and cooking purposes, and frequent scarcity of tents were sure to take their toll.[1] The soldiers often had to build their own huts for winter quarters, and it is not surprising that frigid January weather found part of Washington's force at Valley Forge without housing.[2] One of the most severe winters on record broke upon his army at Morristown while some of the men were still living in brush shelters.[3] The lack of accommodations for the sick was a most distressing circumstance. Within three months of the outbreak of war, many had died merely for want of beds to lie on.[4] "The number of sick is incredible," wrote Philip Schuyler from Ticonderoga two months later, "and I have very little assistance to afford them."[5]

Thus the melancholy story begins, and thus it continues throughout the war. It has been calculated that by October 12, 1775, 937 men had been discharged from Schuyler's army because of sickness, 150 were languishing in the hospital at Lake George, and some 150 more were waiting to enter it.[6] The health and morale of Arnold's force on the way to Quebec were unimpaired until after he left the Kennebec, but then a variety of maladies soon rendered half the men more fit for the hospital than for the field. Smallpox later appeared and completed the demoralization.[7] "Poor attendance; no bed to lie on; no medicine to take," commented one sufferer in the camp before Quebec.[8] When General John Thomas took command there in 1776, he found nearly half the men sick and all clamoring to go home.[9] In fact, sickness practically ruined the northern army at this period.[10] Next August, Gates confessed that the smallpox was the enemy he dreaded most. The troops at Ticonderoga nearly mutinied for want of medicines to relieve their indescribable suffering.[11] Wayne called the hospital there a "House of Carnage."[12]

While in New York Washington's army suffered greatly from disease and a high mortality rate. In early August, 1776, over 3000 were incapacitated out of a total of some 17,000. Lack of tents during protracted rains helped to swell the number of patients.[13] There were regiments without a single field officer capable of doing duty. By September at least a fourth of the men were sick.[14] Mismanagement and graft added immeasurably to their distress.[15] So terribly was the army demoralized by such conditions that widespread reports of the suffering almost paralyzed recruiting at the end of the year.[16] Poor diet and lack of accommodations, along with failure to inoculate recruits against smallpox, continued to menace army health in the following months.[17] Neglected men were tormented with the itch until many were unfit for duty from this cause alone.[18] Crowded conditions in the hospitals produced shocking mortality.[19] At Valley Forge a little straw would have saved the lives of many who languished on the cold ground.[20] Vermin fairly ate up the ragged, emaciated men.[21] The sick were lamentably neglected to the end of the war.[22]

In regions remote from Washington's headquarters the health conditions were often still more deplorable than those just described. At one time 5000 men were left at Peekskill without a general hospital, many of them naked, sick, or convalescent.[23] In early November, 1777, patients at Charleston, S. C., were still in miserable huts.[24] Dr. John Cochran reported that the Albany hospital in March, 1781, was entirely destitute of all kinds of supplies except for a little bad vinegar, and that the patients were frequently without bread or beef for days at a time, so that the doctor was obliged to permit such of them as could walk to beg provisions among the townspeople.[25] William Davies late in 1780 reported extreme distress at Chesterfield, Va., for lack of a physician and hospital accommodations.[26] Throughout the following year there were complaints in Virginia of lack of doctors, medicines, and shelter.[27] There was actually no hospital in the State except a temporary, unfinished log house, with a roof that leaked like a sieve, so that the sick might almost as well have been out of doors.[28]

Greene's southern campaign admirably illustrates this phase of our subject. The hospitals at Salisbury, he reported soon after his arrival in the South, were suffering for want of provisions and everything else that was necessary to make the patients' situation tolerable. He had found the hospital at Charlotte in a condition "shocking to humanity."[29] The entire hospital department, he wrote soon afterward, was in deplorable condition.[30] Again in April he insisted that Congress give attention to the intolerable situation. But the uselessness of such appeals is indicated by a glimpse of the hospitals next September, still "without Medicines, & destitute of Stores, and every Article necessary to render the Sick Comfortable."[31] It is needless to continue the story. No tents, no medicines, few doctors, inadequate shelter; hospital patients wretched for lack of soap and clothing; dysentery, rheumatism, and fever raging among the troops—such is the record to the end.[32] The suffering was incredible. For want of surgeons and supplies, declared Greene, numbers of soldiers were practically eaten up by maggots, and so perished miserably.[33] He maintained that the amount of sickness in the South was over five times that in the North in proportion to numbers engaged, and that the cases were more often fatal.[34]

There is no escape from the conclusion that deplorable health conditions constituted a serious hazard to army morale from first to last.

### WAGES[1]

Even before serious inflation occurred, army wages were inadequate. Common civilian labor commanded much better pay. Such was the discontent over deduction of a fourth of the six and two-thirds dollars a month to pay for the men's clothing that Congress had to legislate against soldiers' selling their clothes to eke out their wages.[2] William Heath, Greene, and Washington warned Congress early in the war that the troops could not buy necessities. With prices already rising, wages in 1776 were barely sufficient to keep the men in clothes, much less to support the families of those who were married.[3] Before the end of the year, artillerists had to be promised a 25% increase in order to keep any of them in the army.[4]

Currency depreciation became serious by the end of 1778. Thereafter Congress found it impossible to keep up with army needs. The troops found necessities insufferably expensive.[5] The dilemma was particularly galling to married men, who worried over the fate of their families, and to officers, who struggled in vain to keep up appearances.[6] Wages of officers were too low in relation to those of privates, and far below the British standard.[7] By 1780 an officer's traveling expense for one day almost equaled a month's pay,[8] the price of a good horse equaled ten years' wages,[9] and a Colonel found his laundry bill exceeding his entire wages.[10] Officers gradually consumed their private fortunes and sank into poverty.[11] While friends in civilian life amassed fortunes, they were compelled to implore, half naked, for consideration from Congress.[12] Upward of fifty officers in Greene's division at Valley Forge resigned in a single day because their families at home were suffering.[13] By April, 1778, officers were asking Washington for leave to resign at the rate of two or three a day, and he called desperately for action to save the army.[14]

In August, 1780, Washington again reported a serious situation. Wages had not only fallen far below the price level, but were so hopelessly in arrears that mutiny was imminent.[15] Payment of wages throughout the war, in fact, was notoriously slow and uncertain. Hardly a day passed when Washington did not receive grievous complaints on this score.[16] The situation in Northern and Southern Departments was, if possible, worse than that in the army under his immediate command. In 1781 the Virginia troops had not received a farthing of pay for two years.[17] At the close of that year Greene complained that he had not been furnished with a shilling in specie since he assumed command.[18] With his army well-nigh desperate, he was forced to make unauthorized drafts upon Robert Morris to keep his troops together, and even so he was harassed by the sight of men selling their few clothes, the sick dying for want of cash to buy from the farmers, and officers leaving unpaid debts wherever they went.[19] Such pledges as Congress and the States made to remedy the situation were held lightly. The patriot troops went home after the war thoroughly disillusioned and with nothing but paper promises in their pockets.[20]

# ☆ II ☆

# *Psychological Factors*

## PROVINCIALISM

Revolutionary patriotism was distinctly provincial in character. The loyalty of the average patriot was not to the United States, but to his State. Soldiers did their best when they felt that they were fighting for their own province. The militia considered themselves primarily a local defensive force, and resented any attempt to draw them away from their own firesides. Even when immediate danger threatened, militia troops often could not realize that their best defense was to march at once to meet the invader. It was with difficulty that the States were persuaded to relax their laws confining militia to service within the province.[1]

Sectional jealousies constituted a menace to morale. John Stark sulked against Congress and hated New York with a perfect hatred: only Burgoyne's threat to his native New Hampshire stirred him to effective action.[2] When southern members of Congress suggested that Continental troops be used to suppress the New Hampshire insurgents and to dissolve Seth Warner's defiant regiment, James Duane sagely observed that "it would not have been wise to hazard either of them."[3] Even in the palmy days of

1775 such dangerous friction developed between Ethan Allen and Benedict Arnold at Crown Point that Arnold's men freely charged the Green Mountain Boys with threatening his life.[4] The fiery Arnold was further embroiled with the Massachusetts Provincial Congress to the point of open defiance of the latter's authority.[5] Interstate rivalries in Richard Montgomery's army in 1775 were hardly less serious.[6] In 1776 Carter Braxton argued against declaring independence on the ground that 800 New Englanders were in arms in the Wyoming Valley, and it appeared that "the Continent would be torn in pieces by Intestine Wars and Convulsions."[7] The garrison in the valley had to be replaced with troops belonging neither to Pennsylvania nor to Connecticut.[8]

Local prejudices were by no means confined to the militia. To encourage recruiting, Washington had to promise on at least one occasion that particular regiments of Continental troops would not for the time being have to leave their State.[9] Deserters from the Continental Army were much more likely to rejoin their regiments when they were told that the remainder of their service would be confined to their home districts.[10] Washington's early hope of forming a truly national army was doomed to disappointment. His troops at Cambridge were thrown into excitement when they heard that the generals were to be chosen by Congress and provincial distinctions abolished.[11] Friction developed when southern men joined his army: epithets of "Yankee" and "Buckskin" quickly flew back and forth, and jealousy arose between New England and southern colonels.[12] Greene feared the consequences of the fierce sectional hatreds that prevailed.[13] Washington at New York and John Sullivan in the North appealed to officers and men to forget local attachments.[14] The worried Commander-in-Chief warned that nothing could assist the enemy more effectually than interstate jealousies, and that the success of the common cause hinged upon the preservation of harmony. He went so far as to threaten with disgraceful dismissal any officer or private who continued to stir up jealousies.[15]

The extent of the problem is indicated by the fact that Washington himself at first harbored prejudice against Massachusetts. Bay State men, he thought, were on the whole "the most indifferent kind of People." He conceded that the privates would fight well if properly officered, though they were "an exceeding dirty and nasty people," but he insisted that their officers were responsible for the defeat at Bunker Hill.[16] If a man of Washington's breadth had to overcome such prejudices, it is no matter for surprise that the average soldier was never able to rise above them. Officers from different States could not tolerate one another in the same regiment.[17] Toward the end of 1776 Washington had to confess that his constant efforts to discourage local attachments had failed. The most he could hope to do was to use State rivalries as a leverage for recruiting the new army.[18]

The States continued to have a large part in army administration, and resulting differences in pay and supplies produced much friction.[19] Provincial jealousies precluded any satisfactory system of appointing officers. The whole matter of appointments and promotions was like a smoldering fire ready to flare up at any time.[20] Provincial attachments of troops to officers almost tore the northern army to pieces right in the face of Burgoyne's invasion.[21] Such dangerous localism diminished very little as the war progressed. In 1778 Washington was compelled to ask a council of war how best to handle a junction of his force with the northern army at White Plains so that sectional strife might be avoided. The board of officers decided that the troops of each State should camp together and should be arranged geographically in accordance with the alignment of States along the seacoast, with no post of honor being implied.[22] In 1780 the Commander-in-Chief still doubted whether he had one army or thirteen.[23]

### DISCIPLINE

At the outbreak of hostilities the colonies had no regular army. Experienced officers were few. The militia had little or no training. Thus the bulk of the army consisted of raw recruits—"a mixed multitude," Washington said, "under very little discipline, order, or Government."[1] A fiercely independent spirit among both officers and men, amounting almost to anarchy, hindered all efforts to transform the mob into a real army.[2] Officers were compelled to indulge their troops to a dangerous degree lest re-enlistment be discouraged and the new year find the country without an army of any kind.[3] In September, 1775, Schuyler's army was on the verge of mutiny.[4] Arnold's force destined for Quebec was in little better condition.[5] Congress soon realized that the military code was inadequate, but the revision effected in 1776 made only slight improvement.[6] It was not until 1778 that Steuben was employed as Inspector General.[7] He was able to improve the drilling and maneuvering of the troops, but could do little to change the prevailing insubordination.[8]

Washington was naturally a strict disciplinarian, but he had to adapt himself as best he could to the situation as he found it. Mere severity would not solve the problem. Several executions for serious offenses left him unconvinced of their deterrent effect.[9] We find him pardoning such crimes as desertion and assaulting an officer with intent to kill.[10] The death penalty, in fact, was so often accompanied by a pardon that it was apparently used largely as a threat.[11] Washington was very sparing in orders for actual executions.[12] In view of the difficulty of maintaining an army in any form, it is difficult to see how he could have pursued a different policy.

Despite the efforts of conscientious officers, lawlessness continued to constitute a major problem to the end of the war. American soldiers, though patient under hardships, were too deeply immersed in Revolutionary ideas of liberty and democracy to tolerate strict military discipline. The leveling spirit was so strong that proper distinctions of rank were almost impossible to establish.[13] Soldiers' "notions of liberty," as Greene expressed it, were "nothing short of licentiousness."[14] Montgomery was appalled at finding himself almost powerless to control men who, he complained, "carry the spirit of freedom into the field, and think for themselves."[15] Baron von Steuben soon noted the contrast between the American spirit and that of Prussia or France. In Europe, he recalled, the officer said to his subordinate, " 'Do this,' and he doeth it." In America, one had to say, " 'This is the reason why you ought to do that:' and then he does it."[16] To Benjamin Franklin he confided: "We want, above all, the true meaning of the words liberty, independence, etc., that the child may not make use of them against his father, or the soldier against his officer."[17] Washington, though lacking the inspector's European experience, was forced to a like conclusion.[18] Officers of an entire corps might defy their commandant and block his plans.[19] Numbers of these "Enemies to Discipline," as Wayne aptly called them, abused both their men and their superiors, defied the orders of the Commander-in-Chief himself, and in general proposed to do as they pleased.[20] The South was pestered by defiant officers who refused to join their regiments, but instead led guerrilla bands about the country and committed grievous excesses.[21]

The mistaken policy of short-term enlistments helped to perpetuate insubordination to the end of the war. Officers would get their men into shape only to have them replaced by raw recruits. "Not a continental officer, I fear," said Alexander Scammell, "will be left in the field, if he must every six months, become a drill sergeant."[22] In 1780 Washington confessed that too many orders were of no avail. "They are read by some," he wrote, "only heard of by others, and inaccurately attended to by all, whilst by a few, they are totally disregarded."[23] His cool reflection after five years of war was that discipline had been practically ruined by continual changes in army personnel.[24]

The use of militia greatly aggravated the problem. The constant sifting of these raw troops through the army threatened the subversion of all discipline whatsoever. They were subject to the Continental Articles of War only when acting in actual conjunction with regular troops, and then only with important exceptions.[25] The States were almost totally unable to discipline their troops. Indeed, they were practically at the mercy of their militia.[26] State governors in the South admitted that militia discipline was nonexistent.[27] Greene well summarized the situation when he said: "With the militia everybody is a general, and the powers of government are so feeble, that it is with the utmost difficulty you can restrain them from plundering one another." The people were not wanting in martial spirit, "but they must go to war in their own way or not at all."[28] Everywhere jealousy was likely to arise when regulars and militia acted together, and the lawlessness of the latter was sure to demoralize the entire army.[29] As the war progressed, Washington used his militia in so far as possible at detached points.[30]

Political interference was another complicating factor. Congress hampered army leaders by vexatious restrictions, and sometimes reached into the army to pardon convicted soldiers.[31] State influence was always a disruptive element.[32] Civilian mismanagement was discouraging.[33] Furthermore, there was the inevitable contingent of female hangers-on, many of them evil in character and all of them more or less of a problem.[34] City life was sure to demoralize the men, insomuch that Washington carefully kept his army from the vicinity of Philadelphia.[35] The policy of keeping isolated detachments in service and of parceling out the troops among various locations for winter quarters was another source of mischief.[36] Intoxication was also a potent cause of negligence and disorder.[37]

We are dealing, then, with the morale of soldiers who were intensely individualistic, always more or less insubordinate, and often mutinous. Weak discipline does not mean that morale was correspondingly weak. The independent spirit that defied regimentation was the very spirit which, when turned against the enemy, made for dogged resistance in a rebellion. But insubordination did prove to be extremely discouraging to the best army officers. It meant too that leaders had to control and inspire the soldiery by personal influence rather than by mere regimentation. Furthermore, in the crisis of battle, morale was much more precarious among poorly trained men than among British regulars.[38] And lastly, insubordination combined dangerously with the hardships suffered by the soldiers to produce mutinies which threatened at times to wreck the patriot army entirely.

The most serious of these mutinies are so well known to history that a detailed account of them here is unnecessary. But we may well examine their causes and their significance, and give some attention to the minor outbreaks. The sources show that uprisings of any importance occurred in the patriot army only when the men were suffering intolerable hardships and felt themselves to be victims of injustice.[39] Americans have always shown strong prejudice against a standing army as a menace to liberty—an attitude typically Anglo-Saxon and not without justification, but carried to such extremes that it came near ruining the Revolutionary cause.[40] The public never appreciated the army as the first essential in the war. Congress and the States, despite Washington's repeated assurances that the army properly used would prove the first bulwark of liberty, pursued a suspicious, parsimonious policy from first to last.[41]

There were a few occasions when patriotic citizens donated funds to relieve needy soldiers.[42] But in general the populace was indifferent.[43] Profiteering flaunted in the face of the suffering soldier the sordid ingratitude of the public: it began when farmers brought produce into the camp before Boston, and flourished to the end in spite of laws and army orders against it. Manufacturers, merchants, and tavernkeepers fleeced the soldiers.[44] Shoes were sometimes so inferior that they lasted but a few days. Blankets turned up one-fourth the proper size.[45] Baron de Kalb estimated that the contractors made 50% on every contract.[46] Washington wished that speculators might hang on gallows five times as high as Haman's.[47] Illicit trade with the enemy flourished while the patriot army went cold and hungry.[48] Not only did the States neglect their troops, but, by vexatious restrictions, they made it almost impossible for the army to supply itself by impressment.[49] Stark feared to send a company of men to Albany lest the citizens there might clap half of them into jail and force the other half to keep them there.[50] Thus popular suspicion and ingratitude added immeasurably to the suffering of the soldiers, and a sense of injustice rankled in their bosoms until they came to hate the civil authorities.[51]

Under such conditions it is not surprising that mutinies occurred and that they became more serious as the war progressed. While unfulfilled promises tantalized the army, the best of officers found it impossible at times to keep their men in hand. Minor outbreaks became alarmingly frequent in 1777, especially among the New York militia.[52] Early in the year Wayne acted with vigor to suppress a mutiny which began at Ticonderoga when a rifle company shouldered arms and packs in an effort to go home. He leveled a pistol at the breast of a sergeant, chastised a private on the spot, arrested a captain as an abettor, and thus summarily quelled the rising.[53] In November, Enoch Poor's brigade of New Englanders, who were behind many months in their pay and who lacked supplies, refused to march from Fishkill to join the main army in Pennsylvania. A captain killed one mutineer, and was himself slain before the officers restored order. Ebenezer Learned's brigade at New Windsor was induced to march only by payment of some wages due.[54]

Thereafter the situation became steadily more serious. The army at Providence experienced two mutinies in the winter of 1778-1779 because of inadequate pay.[55] Next spring it suffered two more when flour became exhausted.[56] A mutiny of the troops guarding the Saratoga prisoners at Charlottesville, Va., which was nipped in the bud, was likewise due to lack of supplies.[57] When bread and vegetables were scarce at West Point late in 1779, half of Albert Pawling's corps decided to march off to see the governor, but were dissuaded from doing so before the troops ordered against them arrived on the scene.[58] On January 1, 1780, sixty of the Massachusetts troops at the same place actually marched away, claiming that their terms had expired, but were brought back without resistance.[59] A few weeks later a rising at Lancaster on account of failure to pay money promised in lieu of clothing was squelched by clapping the leader into irons.[60] In the spring, lack of pay and clothing induced 31 men at Ft. Schuyler to rise in arms and start for Oswagachee. Thirteen were slain on the evening of the second day when Lieut. John Hardenberg and a party of Oneidas who were pursuing them returned the fire of 16 of the fugitives at Grand River.[61] In 1781 mutiny occurred in Moses Hazen's regiment, which had been much neglected and had unwisely been sent up to Albany to withstand Tory influence while the men were unpaid. The 1st New York Regiment followed suit in July, with resulting bloodshed.[62] Stark's men at Saratoga, so naked that only 36 out of two regiments were fit for duty, rose in December, and were put down by loyal officers.[63] Such outlying posts were sadly neglected. William Irvine found the Ft. Pitt garrison in such deplorable condition that the troops scarcely resembled white men, and were in a chronically mutinous condition.[64] The Virginia militia in 1781, fed on spoiled meat and ruled under Governor Thomas Jefferson with the utmost laxity, were as unmanageable as those in New York under Governor George Clinton.[65]

Fortunately Washington was able until 1780 to avoid serious trouble in the army under his immediate command, although he was obliged to call out part of his troops at Cambridge to take 24 riflemen in hand, and very nearly had serious difficulty at Valley Forge.[66] His chief trouble was with the Connecticut line. That State flagrantly neglected its troops. It failed to redress their grievances even after a mutiny in Ebenezer Huntington's brigade late in 1778.[67] Such parsimony, along with the extreme shortage of provisions at Morristown in 1780, produced one of the most alarming mutinies of the war. Two regiments assembled on their parade one evening (May 25) to march away in a body, and long expostulation on the part of Return J. Meigs and two Pennsylvania colonels, backed up by a threat of force, was required to quiet them. Lack of pay, failure to make up the depreciation in wages, and hunger were their main grievances. Washington, much alarmed over the danger of a general spread of insubordination, wrote desperate appeals to Congress and the Board of War and to Governor Trumbull in an effort to secure supplies.[68] But in 1781 the situation of the men was still worse, and the apathy of the State was more maddening than ever.[69] In May, 1782, another mutiny was discovered before it came to a head, and one plotter was sentenced to death.[70]

Greene was able to take his longsuffering men through the southern campaign of 1781 with no mutinous behavior. But in 1782 a force of Pennsylvania troops who joined him fresh from the northern mutinies of 1781 stirred up the little army to a fever of resentment over the neglect it had suffered from the State of South Carolina and from Congress. Pay and clothing and rum were lacking, provisions were irregular and of poor quality, and the postponement of peace made the men restive. By prompt execution of the Pennsylvania sergeant who was apparently the ringleader, and by sending several officers and privates of both the Pennsylvania and Maryland lines to Salisbury for employment in the laboratory, Greene effectually suppressed an exceedingly dangerous movement.[71] All his precautions, however, failed to control a body of 100 cavalry encamped on the Congaree River. Desperate for lack of pay, provisions, and forage, the corps took its departure in May, 1783, and went to Virginia.[72] The men at Georgetown insisted that they were unjustly detained, and a large part of that regiment also left camp.[73] A mutiny among the Maryland troops was suppressed with great difficulty, and a gathering storm in the Virginia line was averted only by arresting the sergeants.[74] The southern army, in short, got almost completely out of hand before the long-delayed demobilization occurred.

But the most extensive and most dangerous mutinies were those in the Pennsylvania and New Jersey lines in 1781 and 1783. The Pennsylvania mutineers left Morristown on January 1, 1781, marched to Princeton, and threatened to go on to Philadelphia. They killed several officers who tried to restore order, but refrained from plunder; and, at Wayne's suggestion, they executed as spies two agents from Sir Henry Clinton who held out strong inducements to join the British. Their refusal to disperse except on their own terms forced the authorities to capitulate. About half of the mutineers were discharged outright, and the rest were furloughed until next April. Washington's first impulse had been to march a sizable detachment from New Windsor to the scene of disorder. But the threat of similar trouble in his own force, and a serious doubt as to whether the bulk of his men would act against their brethren, made him pause. He finally decided merely to keep a thousand men in readiness.[75] The outcome of this affair was ominous indeed. Discerning officers realized that failure to suppress the mutiny in summary fashion had shaken the whole structure of army discipline to its very foundations.[76]

The causes of the mutiny were well known. A dispute over terms of enlistment, and the presence of foreign-born soldiers in the line complicated the situation, but it was everywhere recognized that the fundamental cause was the excessive hardships endured by the army.[77] In spite of this fact, the civil authorities failed to act.[78] The whole problem, as usual, was left to Washington.

Fortunately the army dealt with the next mutinies so decisively that the crumbling foundations of discipline were restored. When the New Jersey detachment at Pompton, fired by liquor and by the news of the Pennsylvania rising, mutinied on January 20 to the number of about 200, Washington was in no mood for trifling. At considerable risk, in view of his scanty supplies and the general unrest, he marched a force of some 600 of his best troops from West Point under Robert Howe, forbade all compromise, and within a week had suppressed the mutiny by executing two of the leaders.[79] Furthermore, he took all possible precautions to deal with any further trouble.[80] It was not long in coming. In May, twelve men of the Pennsylvania line at York stepped forward and persuaded the men not to march to Virginia, on the ground that the promises made them after their first mutiny had not been kept. Wayne acted with energy. Seven mutineers met their death on the spot, and the other five were hanged soon afterward. It was bloody work, but essential to the preservation of the army.[81]

The last major mutiny, also in the Pennsylvania line, occurred at the end of the war when most of the army had disbanded. Throughout the months of waiting for demobilization, discontent over the failure to make final provision for the army had seethed like a cauldron.[82] At last, on June 17, 1783, the lid blew off. Eighty men marched to Philadelphia, where their number was swelled to about 500 by the rising of the men barracked there. For days the civil authorities were practically at their mercy. Congress fled to Princeton. But Washington soon had 1,500 men—practically his whole force—in motion under Robert Howe to quell the uprising. Before the arrival of these troops Arthur St. Clair and the Executive Council of Pennsylvania managed to get the situation under control.[83]

In the light of the sources, it must be admitted that Revolutionary troops were individualistic to the point of lawlessness, but it may also be said that on the whole they were loyal to the patriot cause and were driven to mutiny only by excessive hardship and civilian neglect. In the critical closing years of the war an able, unscrupulous leader might conceivably have taken advantage of the situation to establish a dictatorship. Such a disaster was averted by the ability of Washington and by his devotion to republican ideals.

### BEHAVIOR IN ACTION

An important factor in Revolutionary army morale was the patriot's feeling of inferiority before better trained British regulars. In only one respect did the American feel himself superior to his opponent in battle—namely, in marksmanship.[1] Washington took great satisfaction in this one asset, to which he attributed the heavy British casualties during skirmishes.[2] But the patriot's confidence in his gunnery was offset during the first half of the war by his fear of the British bayonet. Until Steuben introduced bayonet practice in 1778, the army used the weapon very little, and this inferiority was no small factor in producing the awe which the redcoats inspired. In 1781 the British still boasted of victories won with the bayonet, and Washington must still urge his men to give thrust for thrust.[3]

Fear of the bayonet is inevitable among raw troops, and points to lack of training as a most serious problem. Morale is at best a fickle, unpredictable phenomenon, and with poorly trained men it is doubly precarious. Soldiers who were frightened by the mere sight of panic-stricken women and children running about and shrieking in New York City could hardly be expected to stand against a trained enemy in the open field.[4] Like all raw troops, moreover, they never feared for their heads, but thought only of their legs. "Shelter them and they will fight forever," said Israel Putnam. Washington was convinced that if his men were behind a parapet their skill with the gun would enable them to give a good account of themselves, but that they would not march up to a work or fight exposed in a plain.[5]

His fears confirmed by the behavior of his army before a vastly superior force at New York, Washington warned Congress of the presumption of drawing inexperienced men into open ground against their superiors in numbers and discipline. He had never spared pick and spade, and yet had not found that dogged courage even in defending strong posts which was essential if the army were to derive the greatest benefit from fortification.[6] Hence the little advantage gained at Harlem Heights on September 16, 1776, gave a tremendous lift to morale. The men found that resolution and good leadership could prevail against a foe that had inspired such dread.[7] The battles of Germantown and Saratoga had similar value.[8] But it is doubtful whether Americans ever completely overcame their early sense of inferiority. Steuben complained that the prevailing prepossession in favor of the British military system obliged him to mold the army code to English forms.[9]

Under such conditions it is not surprising that cases of cowardice mar the record, especially before Steuben improved discipline in 1778. Alarming instances appeared during the Canadian campaign of 1775.[10] Next year, during the New York campaign, Washington was mortified by further examples.[11] As late as 1780 he declared that it was not unusual for men in action to expend their powder at too great a distance, and then to make their want of it an excuse for quitting the field.[12] Greene's fight near Camden in 1781 was lost in spite of a most promising beginning because of the misbehavior of some of the Maryland troops.[13]

The use of raw recruits, especially militia, inevitably produced general panic on more than one occasion. Arnold characterized the demoralization of both officers and men after the repulse at Quebec as "amazing." Upward of 100 of them set off instantly for Montreal, and only the greatest efforts induced the rest to take a stand. The panic soon subsided; but, had the British improved their opportunity, the American army would have been ruined.[14] When a British fleet appeared and Sir Guy Carleton made a cautious sally, panic again seized the troops under Thomas. Muskets were thrown away. Loaded cannon, baggage, and stores were abandoned. Even hospital patients staggered off.[15] The appearance of William Howe's army at Kip's Bay in 1776 drove Washington's men from New York in such a rout that the utmost efforts of the Commander-in-Chief could not restore order. "I have often read and heard of . . . cowardice," William Smallwood later declared, "but hitherto have had but a faint idea of it . . . I could wish the transactions of this day blotted out of the annals of America. Nothing appeared but fright, disgrace, and confusion."[16] Men ran off without firing a shot. Washington called their conduct "disgraceful and dastardly."[17]

Though the patriots many times redeemed themselves by gallant conduct, yet the danger of panic remained. Officers were known to station trustworthy men in the rear during a battle with orders to shoot any soldier who fled.[18] It took more than threats and courts martial, however, to insure coolness on the part of poorly trained men pitted against European regulars. At Germantown Washington was again mortified to see his men, apparently confused by a fog, break into a disorderly retreat on the very verge of victory;[19] while at Camden the unreasoning panic and precipitate flight of the entire army, from Gates on down, were so disgraceful that the episode has become proverbial.[20]

Gates' conduct points to the fact that unworthy officers were responsible for much of the misconduct in battle. Washington ascribed the failure at the Cedars to the cowardly conduct of two officers, and, after repeated disappointments, went so far as to say in 1777 that no well-officered regiment in his army had ever been found guilty of cowardice.[21] Greene likewise blamed one of his officers for the failure at Hobkirk's Hill in 1781.[22] Frequent convictions of officers on charges of cowardice tend to confirm this opinion. Timothy Bedel and Isaac Butterfield, who surrendered at the Cedars; Christopher Gardiner, who deserted his post at Bunker Hill; Mordecai Buckner and William Work, who were tried at Morristown, and Lieutenant John Waterman, guilty of cowardice near White Plains in 1777, were among the numerous officers dismissed for such misbehavior from 1775 to 1778; and many others were disciplined in various ways throughout the war for similar offenses.[23] There must have been many cases also of officers who, like Thomas Conway, were strongly suspected of cowardice but were not brought to trial.[24]

The disaster at Camden also illustrates the fickleness of militia on the battlefield. By far the largest part of Gates' army was militia who had never been in action, and the great majority of these untried troops fled without firing a shot. The firm behavior of the regulars at the same time formed a striking contrast.[25] Untrained men nearly made another Camden of the battle of Guilford Court House early in 1781.[26] Such risks would never have been taken if the advice of men like Washington had been heeded. From the time that two brigades of New England militia fled disgracefully from a small party of the enemy at Harlem (September, 1776), the Commander-in-Chief had denounced the whole militia system.[27] Greene believed that if the untrained men at Ft. Lee had obeyed orders, not a man there would have been captured,[28] and he was convinced that Ft. Washington could have been defended had the garrison consisted of regulars instead of a large proportion of panic-stricken militia.[29] During the skirmish at Boundbrook (April 13, 1777) the militia guarding a ford of the Raritan deserted without giving the commander the least notice of the approach of the enemy, who thereupon captured almost all his papers and came near taking his whole force.[30] In the battle against William Tryon at Norwalk (1779) the militia retreated in disorder, leaving the regulars to do the fighting.[31] The total failure of Massachusetts' militia expedition to Penobscot should have disillusioned naive believers in "a well regulated militia."[32]

There were times when the militia fought well, especially in conjunction with trained troops. The Philadelphia militia behaved bravely at Princeton.[33] Irregular troops were often useful in small parties to harass the enemy.[34] Particularly in the fierce guerrilla warfare in the Carolinas did the militia of Marion, Sumter, and other leaders render valuable service.[35] Furthermore, the way in which the populace was able to rise against an invader who struck too far into the interior constituted no small factor in American success. While they were incapable of sustained action and unfit for regular warfare, yet many a British general attempted to penetrate the country only to find the farmers swarming angrily about him until they halted his progress. Gage, Howe, Cornwallis, Burgoyne, and Arnold all found this out to their sorrow. The battles of Bennington, Oriskany, Saratoga, King's Mountain, and the Cowpens, to say nothing of numberless small engagements, are cases in point.[36] Washington greatly appreciated the service of the militia in 1779-1780 during British coastal raids. Particularly impressive was the success of the New Jersey militia, who had been organized by Gov. William Livingston and were able to hold Knyphausen's 5,000 men in check until Washington could march from Morristown to cope with the situation.[37] Arnold invaded Virginia only to find himself pestered beyond measure by swarms of angry patriots. So furiously did they buzz about the ears of the detested traitor that, after burning Richmond, he was compelled to retreat to Portsmouth.[38] Cornwallis became so weary of trying to fight the whole countryside as well as Greene's army that he aptly called the Carolinas a hornets' nest.[39]

It is, in fact, pleasant to discover that among both militia and regular troops the sources reveal many more cases of bravery than of cowardice. Obviously this is due in part to the tendency of officers to play up their successes. But this does not destroy the impression that American soldiers, when engaged with troops of comparable training, were as courageous as the British. The Earl of Balcarras, one of Burgoyne's best officers, decided that Americans were far from contemptible on the battlefield, and in this conclusion the Earl of Harrington concurred.[40] Another of His Majesty's officers wrote sadly after Bunker Hill of the heavy British losses, and confessed: "We have, indeed, learned one melancholy truth, which is, that the Americans, if they were equally well commanded, are full as good soldiers as ours."[41] It is apparent that the bravery of such experienced officers as Prescott, Putnam, Stark, and Knowlton was the deciding factor in the surprising record of the patriots on that occasion.[42] Gage was convinced that "the rebels are not the despicable rabble too many have supposed them to be," and opined that "a military spirit, encouraged among them for a few years past, joined with an uncommon degree of zeal and enthusiasm," accounted for the phenomenon.[43]

Arnold's letters, written in the bitterness of defeat, acknowledged the intrepidity of many of his officers and men in the desperate attempt on Quebec.[44] Indeed, as Justin Smith reminds us, the wonder is not that the attack failed but rather that men would dare to venture at all into such death-traps.[45] The summer of 1776 witnessed the courageous attack on Three Rivers, where Wayne, as often, distinguished himself; the notable attack on Lord Dunmore at Gwin's Island; and the brave stand of Lord Stirling's brigade on Long Island, ended only by the overwhelming superiority of British numbers.[46] Later in the year came the exhibition of bravery at Harlem Heights which elicited such warm praise from Washington, Ritzema's and Smallwood's cool defense at White Plains,

Colonel Rawlings' spirited defense of the pass north of Ft. Washington, and the eager attack which overpowered the Hessians at Trenton.[47] The year 1777 was signalized by Bennington, Arnold's desperate valor at Stillwater, and the notable defense of Ft. Mifflin. The four hours' hand-to-hand fight against Burgoyne especially impressed English historian Charles Stedman; he stated it convinced every one of the ability of American troops to sustain an attack in the open field "with the intrepidity, the spirit, and the coolness of veterans."[48] Actions such as Monmouth, where Wayne and Washington especially distinguished themselves; Newport, where less than a third of Sullivan's force had seen previous action; Wayne's brilliant surprise of Stony Point; and southern exploits like King's Mountain, the Cowpens, and Eutaw Springs, stand out among many engagements, great and small, which exhibited American spirit at its best during the remaining years of the war.[49]

### FLUCTUATIONS IN MORALE

The history of the Revolution reveals an initial outburst of tremendous enthusiasm, followed by a rapid cooling off as hopes for a quick victory were dashed to the ground. Thereafter the morale of the patriot army fluctuated widely in response to a number of factors, including the uncertainty caused by short terms of enlistment, the changing European situation, the fortunes of battle, the necessity of using a Fabian policy during much of the war, and the growing weariness as the conflict dragged on. An examination of these factors will help to make the situation clear.

The "Spirit of 1775" would unquestionably fit the facts much better than the traditional phrase, the "Spirit of 1776." It is difficult to determine exactly when the latter term came into general use, but apparently it was after the close of the war. Contemporary references to the early enthusiasm uniformly point to 1775 rather than 1776 as the ideal year.[1] Only the year 1775 witnessed unalloyed enthusiasm on the part of the patriots. Lexington and Concord and the siege of Boston, along with the early successes in the South, convinced the Whigs that victory was a matter of course. But 1776 was marred by news of Quebec and the demoralization of the retreat from New York.[2] News of Lexington and Concord started thousands of volunteers toward Boston. In poured the New Hampshire militia under Stark, the Connecticut volunteers under Putnam (who, Roman-like, had left his plow in the furrow), and the Rhode Island men under Greene, until the army about Boston quickly outnumbered Gage's force at least three to one. So hot was the fervor of rebellion that, when Congress authorized the raising of ten companies of riflemen in Pennsylvania, Virginia, and Maryland for one year, twelve companies appeared before Boston in sixty days. Some of them had marched eight hundred miles.[3] Instead of the 800 men expected, 1430 responded, generally bringing their own rifles. Pecuniary considerations were forgotten.[4] Gage and his officers were dumbfounded.[5] From every side came news of men turning out in overwhelming numbers and with reckless abandon.[6] Congressional plans to raise 100,000 men, Pennsylvania's hopes of putting 20,000 into the field within a month, visions of an entire populace in arms regardless of class or creed—such were the wild dreams of sober Americans in those halcyon spring days.[7] We may well believe that when the "Declaration on the Causes and Necessity of Taking up Arms" was read in camp the troops cheered so lustily as to alarm the enemy on Bunker Hill.[8]

Never again during the Revolution did such morale actuate the American patriot. The enthusiasm declined even sooner than is generally realized. Washington perceived the effervescent character of the morale of those days, and was anxious for a decisive engagement that would satisfy the expectation of quick and easy victory. By September 8th his men were already impatient to go home; on the 21st he was compelled to acknowledge that most of the army was in a state "not far from mutiny." After only five months of war, he feared the actual break-up of his force.[9] In the following weeks he experienced infinite difficulty in recruiting an army for 1776. Officers, he complained, stood off in expectation of promotion, while privates waited to see who their officers would be.[10] "No Troops were ever better provided, or higher paid," he told Schuyler, "yet their Backwardness to enlist for another Year is amazing." He lamented the egregious want of patriotism which threatened to dissolve the army before his very eyes, declaring that the granting of at least a hundred furloughs from each regiment was the only means by which men could be re-enlisted at all.[11] Only 966 men had enlisted by November 19.[12] Thus easily did the Spirit of 1775 evaporate before the prospect of a protracted struggle.

It is evident that the early spirit was based on the illusion that victory would be won by an immediate, decisive stroke. As in the American Civil War, a few months of hostilities without apparent result sufficed to dull the enthusiasm of the multitude.[13] War weariness soon settled down like a pall, and tended to deepen as years passed. By the summer of 1777 the early zeal had pretty well vanished.[14] Attention has already been called to the increasing difficulty of recruiting.[15] Additional evidence of the general decline in ardor appears in the statistics of enlistments throughout the war. Estimates of the militia response from New York, New Jersey, Pennsylvania, and Maryland from 1776 to 1781 show a decline from 22,295 to 3880 in the six years.[16] The number of Continentals forthcoming likewise declined from 46,901 in 1776 to a reluctant 14,256 in 1782.[17]

Along with the disappointed expectations of early victory another factor must be considered—the policy of short terms of enlistment.[18] This make-shift plan exasperated officers like Washington almost to the point of desperation. Accompanied as it was by the prospect of steadily increasing bounties, it provided an irresistible temptation to the soldier to postpone re-enlisting, to demand a furlough, or to quit the army entirely.[19] "Nothing but confusion and disorder reign," wrote Greene, as the inevitable exodus took place on the last day of 1775. The necessity of retaining the guns of the retiring men at prices much below what the owners had paid for them in the previous spring added to the discontent.[20] Yet many carried off their arms, whether public or private property, leaving a shortage for the troops who remained. Discontented officers discouraged recruiting. By February 1, Washington was so appalled at the evils of short terms that he pleaded for recruits for the period of the war even if the price had to be a high bounty.[21]

This policy of short terms continued as a disturbing factor to the end of the war. Montgomery's defeat at Quebec can be attributed in part to the expiring terms of his men which impelled him to a desperate attack contrary to his better judgment; and that is not the only instance of defeat due to this cause.[22] The northern army was angered both at Quebec and Montreal when men were compelled to serve after the expiration of their terms.[23] Time and again throughout the war the armies were thrown into uncertainty and confusion and the generals discouraged by the partial dissolution of the forces when terms of service expired. The men, weary of camp life, rarely stayed after the long-anticipated day arrived, despite the fact that their departure might occur at the most critical stage of a crucial campaign.[24] Comparatively few men enlisted for the period of the war. As late as 1781 the bulk of the army consisted of raw recruits enlisted for terms of from one to three years.[25]

Every conceivable device was used to induce the men to re-enlist. Bounties, special gratuities, and liquor played their part, but with only partial success.[26] Currency depreciation greatly lessened the lure of pecuniary inducements after 1777, and at all times the recruit might abscond with the bounty money.[27] However, men still in the army were much more likely to engage than were those who had gone home.[28] Hence there was widespread resort to furloughs as a means of recruiting. The fact that unreliable men would take both bounty and furlough and then refuse to return made this device a risky one, but it was used with some effect.[29] It was impossible, however, to prevent recurrent crises such as those of 1775, 1776, 1779 and 1780, when the very existence of the army hung in the balance.[30] The unmilitary system also produced chronic discontent. It tempted men to falsify their terms of enlistment, and engendered envy and homesickness in the hearts of those who must remain in camp to watch their more fortunate friends depart joyfully for home.[31] Any attempt at army reorganization which involved the discharge of soldiers before their terms expired, Washington warned, would increase this discontent among the more permanent troops to a dangerous degree.[32]

It is doubtful if there was a more dangerous menace to morale, with the exception of the hardships previously described, than the iniquitous system of short terms. Greene considered it responsible in large measure for all the misfortunes suffered by the patriots.[33] "Instead of securing an army when our money was good and the people were willing," lamented Tench Tilghman (December 22, 1780), "we have lavished sums upon men of an hour whose terms of service have been spent in marching to and from the army, and in their way devouring like locusts all before them."[34] Hamilton went so far as to ascribe to this policy all of America's military misfortunes and three fourths of her civil embarrassments.[35] Washington never thought on the subject, he told Jefferson, without a feeling of horror.[36] Like Hamilton, he attributed all his military reverses to this major error, inasmuch as it produced inferiority to the enemy during most of the war;[37] and in one moment of pessimism he predicted that if it were continued the cause would be lost.[38]

While the psychological effects of short terms were uniformly bad, there was another factor which affected morale now favorably and now adversely—the constantly changing military situation. We have already seen that when hostilities began there was a general expectation that the war would be short.[39] When this hope faded, attention naturally centered about the movement for separation from Britain. As the summer of 1776 approached, the popular imagination was so deeply stirred over the issue that the actual appearance of the Declaration of Independence had an important effect. A skillful crystallization of war aims, it provided the indispensable basis for a popular crusade.[40] Its appearance unquestionably marked the highest point of army morale as well as civilian morale between the spring of 1775 and the battle of Trenton at the end of 1776.[41]

Another important focus for hopes of final victory was the prospect of foreign aid. The need for European alliances was in itself a strong motive for separation from England, and the help received from France before the treaties of 1778 were concluded served to buoy American hopes in a most decided manner.[42] News which reached the army in April, 1778, to the effect that France had recognized the United States also produced a profound impression. When Washington announced it to his officers, he believed no event was ever greeted with keener joy, and declared buoyantly that the glorious news "must put the Independency of America out of all manner of dispute."[43] His army was eager to celebrate the event.[44] Under such circumstances the effect of actual publication of the concluded treaties can be imagined. Their appearance, in fact, was premature because of the general elation.[45] So completely did the European situation distract the minds of the officers during the winter of 1777-1778 that they temporarily forgot their hardships. Thus it contributed definitely to the successful weathering of that difficult season.[46]

Exuberant patriots caught at the alliance as the solution of all their problems until the lack of immediate results gave them a more sober view. Washington himself was doubtful whether, after such a setback, the enemy forces were preparing to evacuate Philadelphia alone or New York and the whole continent as well. It was not until October that he was actually convinced of Britain's intention to remain.[47] Even then he half expected them to leave next spring, and could offer no better reason for their staying than that they had usually acted contrary to all expectation.[48] Greene shared his feeling, and congratulated the country in advance over its victory. "How happy will America be," he exulted, "like a man just free from a racking pain."[49] The Newport affair of 1778, with its strain on Franco-American relations, did not suffice to quench these glowing hopes. "The Arrival of Count D'Estaing to the Southward," wrote Josiah Harmar at West Point (Oct. 9, 1779), "has elevated the Spirits of the whole Army, insomuch that many are sanguine enough to Report & believe that the whole Southern Army is captured."[50]

This exaggerated expectation of decisive results from foreign intervention appears further in the Whig attitude toward Spain. The rumor of Spanish recognition of the United States and of the granting of a loan produced an immediate fall in prices.[51] While Washington warned against expecting too much, he could not avoid indulging in fond hopes.[52] "The declaration of Spain in favor of France has given universal joy to every Whig," he rejoiced, "while the poor Tory droops like a withering flower under a declining Sun."[53] Only in May of next year do we find him pointing out the hollowness of such hopes.[54] However, the disappointment over this will-o'-the-wisp was somewhat offset by the effect of the fresh help which Lafayette secured from France in 1780 and again in 1781.[55] So desperate, indeed, were the patriot prospects in those critical months that the final large-scale co-operation in September, 1781, to capture Cornwallis produced an electrical effect. The landing of 3000 French troops on James Island early that month, wrote one officer, "spread an universal joy amongst our officers and soldiers."[56] The declining military strength of America during the rest of the war produced a dependence upon France that might well be described as abject. Washington had learned well the importance of sea power, and staked the final result of the struggle on the co-operation of the French navy.[57] To France, too, the Whigs had to look in the closing months for the money needed to restore public credit.[58] It is evident that the American army had its eyes constantly on Europe during the Revolution, and that every rumor and offer of help had immediate effects on morale.

Turning now to the mixed effects of events on the battlefield, we are confronted by the fact that a war demanding much retreat and frequent avoidance of pitched battles put a heavy strain on morale. It was difficult for an unwarlike democracy to execute a Fabian policy. Hovering about an invading army and confining its operations require the skill and patience of veterans. Frequent retreats demoralize the best troops.[59] The problem was complicated by the exaggerated importance attached to such events as the failure to conquer Canada and the loss of New York and Philadelphia. The failure of the Canadian campaign effectually completed the discouragement which followed the collapse of early enthusiasm.[60] The victory at Moore's Creek Bridge in February and the British evacuation of Boston in March could not fully restore the spirits of men who felt that the North could not be safe with Canada in enemy hands.[61] Likewise the loss of New York and the long retreat thereafter were disheartening in the extreme. The average soldier could not understand that the city might better have been abandoned to begin with, and instead of rejoicing at the lucky escape of the army from an untenable position, considered that the cause was doomed.[62]

The maintenance of army morale, in fact, bulked large among Washington's reasons for attempting to hold New York. He pointed out the folly of staking everything on the defense of the city, but added significantly that on the other hand to abandon it when some thought it defensible would have a tendency to dispirit the army. The defeat on Long Island had so dampened morale that he was in a quandary. Confessing that a retreating army was beset with difficulties and subjected its leader to reproach, he could not, on the other hand, bring himself to risk a brilliant stroke in the hope of restoring the shattered morale of both soldier and civilian.[63] Heath advised against evacuation because it would dispirit the army and the populace, while Greene urged the opposite on the ground that the army had met with one defeat, the country was in a panic, and a serious loss now might ruin the cause.[64]

Such being the critical state of patriot morale, it is easy to understand Washington's relief when, after abandoning the city, his troops made a courageous stand (September 16) at Harlem

Heights. The skirmish revived drooping spirits so effectively that George Clinton considered it practically equal to a major victory. Joseph Reed declared: "You can hardly conceive the change it has made in our army."[65] The troops had need of all the encouragement available, for the dismal retreat that followed this small success well-nigh shattered American morale. Washington himself experienced the depths of discouragement, especially after the loss of Ft. Washington in November. His shrunken forces were so thoroughly dispirited that he gave up any thought of risking an action.[66] It is estimated that during the retreat to Pennsylvania not 100 men enlisted, while frightened citizens rallied to the enemy by whole companies to take the oath of allegiance.[67] The despairing general wrote that "*if every nerve is not strain'd* to recruit the New Army with all possible expedition, *I think the game is pretty near up.*"[68] It was perhaps the lowest point in morale during the entire Revolution.

The stage was now set for the most dramatic transformation of outlook that occurred during the war. Nothing could have been better calculated to banish despair from patriot hearts than the unexpected strokes at Trenton and Princeton. Both efforts were undertaken with that deliberate purpose,[69] and together they produced an effect almost miraculous.[70] Without doubt Washington's boldness and skill on this occasion saved the cause of the Revolution.[71] Dread of the Hessians was greatly lessened.[72] The New Jersey militia shook off their lethargy and turned out en masse. Army officers were overjoyed, the dejected soldiery smiled once more, congratulations poured in from every quarter, and for a time Washington and his cause basked in sunshine.[73]

The tendency to despair which accompanied the loss of positions of supposedly great importance appears in the story of morale following the fall of Ticonderoga and Ft. Independence.

The value of Ticonderoga was greatly overestimated,[74] and the discouragement after its loss (July, 1777) was widespread and serious.[75] Only in early August did the unreasoning panic show signs of subsiding.[76] Unable to send any considerable reinforcements to oppose Burgoyne, Washington could only call attention to the hopeful swarming of the militia to meet the invader, and attempt to calm the clamoring governors and generals. The worst aspect of the situation, in his opinion, was the unthinking despair which continued in large measure to grip the northern army.[77] It required the arrival of Daniel Morgan's riflemen and of great numbers of militia, as well as the dauntless leadership of Arnold, to restore morale to an effective level.[78]

Both belligerents assigned to Philadelphia an importance far beyond its actual military value.[79] "Philadelphia is the American Diana," wrote Greene; "she must be preserved at all events."[80] Washington had expressed strong concern over its defense in 1776. He feared that the loss of so important a center of supplies would prove almost fatal.[81] Fortunately for the Whigs, the surrender of Burgoyne came just in time to relieve the apprehension produced by the fall of the city. The effect of Saratoga, indeed, was little less striking than that of Trenton and Princeton. "Nothing could fit our troops for action like the joyfull news from Gates," wrote Jedediah Huntington from the camp near Philadelphia.[82] The news caused rejoicing throughout America.[83] Within two months after Howe's entering Philadelphia, Washington could speak of that disappointment with nonchalance. Mere possession of the city, he maintained, brought no solid advantage to British arms.[84] With due allowance for the propagandist motive of this statement, it would still seem that the course of events had produced a more realistic view of British successes.

The discouraging effect of long periods of inactivity became a serious problem as the war progressed. The bleak winter at Valley Forge offers an excellent illustration of such prolonged sinking spells. Even before the army left the vicinity of Philadelphia, Greene remarked that the service was universally disliked, and that he had never seen the army so near dissolving since he had joined it.[85] The statement was possibly exaggerated, and yet it emphasizes the homesickness and eagerness to escape the boredom of winter quarters which regularly showed themselves as cold weather came on. The unusual hardships of the winters at Valley Forge and Morristown aggravated the problem. Steuben rendered a valuable service when he put the shivering men through their drills during the early spring of 1778. Their minds were thus occupied, and more adequate training gave them a solid basis for selfconfidence. It is doubtful whether the battle of Monmouth in June, much as Washington gloried in that event, did more to restore morale.[86]

The effects of inactivity became more pronounced in the North during the latter half of the war when the British turned their attention to the South. Officers deplored "the supineness that constantly seizes our people, when they have been long unmolested," but could suggest no remedy other than small surprise attacks on the enemy.[87] The year 1779 was one of marking time. It was followed by one of the most critical periods of the war. In fact, 1780 without question witnessed the most serious of the prolonged crises of the Revolution. With national finances almost on the rocks, with the army left practically unsupplied except through its own efforts, and with all serious effort paralyzed, it has aptly been called "the blackest year for American hopes." Only French aid enabled the despairing patriots to continue the conflict.[88] Growing army discontent reached the stage of mutiny. Washington was thoroughly alarmed. "There never has been a stage of the War in which the dissatisfaction has been so general or alarming," he warned Congress in April. Short terms, the bounty system, and niggardly provision for the army were bearing their logical fruit. Continued inaction gave time for brooding. Officers resigned right and left, while the rank and file murmured, nursed their grievances, and plotted violence.[89] Lincoln's surrender at Charleston (May 12, 1780) added to the gloom.[90] As if that were not enough, the disaster of Camden occurred in August to dispel almost the last ray of hope.[91]

The first light to break into this darkness was the victory at King's Mountain (October 7, 1780).[92] The situation, however, remained critical for several months more. Greene in the Carolinas and Lafayette and Steuben in Virginia faced almost insuperable obstacles, and the fate of the American cause hung in the balance.[93] The problem in the South during these last years was in many respects the opposite of that in the North, for instead of dulling inactivity there was relentless, exhausting effort on the part of a handful of troops operating against superior forces. For months after his arrival, Greene dared not risk a battle.[94] And yet the need was for further victories like King's Mountain if morale were to be restored. Morgan's fortunate stroke at the Cowpens in January did much to meet the need.[95] Greene's careful leadership, in spite of his inability to win clearcut victories, contributed largely to the same end.[96] It is safe to say that Greene's restoration of southern morale, with the consequent encouragement to Washington's army and to the Whigs everywhere, was indispensable in making the Yorktown campaign possible.[97]

### DEVOTION TO THE CAUSE

But the most striking aspect of American morale was the fortitude displayed through long periods of hardship. Historians have paid enthusiastic tribute to the cheerfulness and hardihood which Arnold's force maintained under the fearful hardships of their march through the Maine woods in 1775.[1] But actual perusal of the men's journals is necessary for full appreciation of the episode. Wading up to their chins at times to push their bateaus, carrying or dragging the craft over roots and rocks and through the mud at the portages, these hardy men suffered much from cold and hunger and fatigue. By October 29, they were breaking ice before them as they waded, and they stood up all one night to dry themselves and keep from freezing.[2] Yet their spirit, except in the case of one Connecticut corps that turned back, surmounted all obstacles. The ghastly faces of the sufferers showed an incredible cheerfulness.[3] The men seemed "fired with more than Hannibalian enthusiasm."[4] Time after time Arnold spoke admiringly of the behavior of both officers and privates. Late in November, although wanting every necessity, they were "as ready as naked men can be, to march wherever they may be required."[5]

So many instances of such fortitude appear in the sources that an attempt to present them is likely to prompt the suspicion that one's judgment has been warped by hero worship. It is impossible, however, to present the picture in its true colors without going further into this aspect. Washington's officers were wont to comment on the cheerfulness with which their men prosecuted wearisome and seemingly useless marches.[6] That such reports were not surprising to the Commander-in-Chief is apparent when one recalls the fidelity of the few who stood by him in the gloomy retreat across New Jersey. Albigence Waldo has left a picture of the ill-clad soldier who, though a raw recruit, maintained cheerfulness in the face of suffering: "If barefoot—he labours thro' the Mud & Cold with a Song in his mouth extolling War & Washington."[7] Observed historian William Lecky: "The time was, indeed, well fitted to winnow the chaff from the grain; and few braver and truer men were ever collected around a great commander than those who remained with Washington during the dreary winter in Valley Forge . . ."[8] John Laurens remarked that the patience of American soldiers astonished foreigners.[9]

The impressions recorded by foreign observers bear out Laurens' statement. Lafayette, his eyes filled with the sight of naked, half-starved men whose feet and legs were frozen black and in some cases had to be amputated, declared that "the patient endurance of both soldiers and officers was a miracle which every moment served to renew."[10] Even the critical Kalb, who was accustomed to denounce all American officers, spoke of the rank and file as troops of such excellence and zeal that it was a shame they were so neglected.[11] When Steuben visited the huts at Valley Forge, he was particularly impressed by the fortitude of the men and their devotion to their cause and their leader. No army in Europe, he told Washington, would hold together under such conditions.[12] Washington himself marveled that such suffering did not incite his army to general mutiny and dispersion.[13] He was, indeed, scarcely exaggerating when he wrote that history could furnish no instance of an army's suffering such extreme hardships with the same degree of patience.[14]

The terrible hardships endured by George Rogers Clark's indomitable band in four days of their march through the flooded Wabash valley in mid-winter are comparable to those of Arnold's men in 1775. But there is no evidence of complaint. Clark insisted that the story was too incredible for any man to believe who did not know him or who had not had a similar experience.[15] In the midst of the rigorous winter at Morristown, Washington observed that both officers and men bore their distress with a patience almost inconceivable.[16] Four days later he ordered Irvine to reconnoiter with a view to an attack on Staten Island, not fearing to send men upon such a venture across the ice despite the fact that they were half starved, poorly clothed, riotous, and prone to rob the people of their substance from sheer necessity.[17] A Congressional committee reported from camp in May, 1780, that the soldiery had endured every conceivable hardship with a fortitude and perseverance which surpassed the expectation of the most sanguine.[18] Charles Thomson thought there was nothing in history to equal it. Notwithstanding the tempting offers of the enemy and the incredible hardships, desertions were comparatively few.[19] Henry Knox referred to such fortitude as "almost superhuman."[20]

One must make due allowance for the propagandist motive behind some of these statements. Yet it is evident that there existed in the American patriot a strain of loyal devotion that impressed both native and foreign observers. Even the Pennsylvania and New Jersey mutinies threw into sharp relief the fidelity of the bulk of the army, whose suffering was almost if not quite as severe as that of the mutineers. Heath found his troops priding themselves on their loyalty while mutiny raged among their brethren, although their own hardships were so great that he doubted whether human nature could long cope with them.[21] Robert Howe's detachment marched through a heavy snow with such alacrity to suppress the New Jersey mutiny that Washington was deeply impressed.[22] Lafayette was unstinted in praise of his men during the difficult campaign in Virginia. He characterized his three battalions of light infantry as "the best troops that ever took the field." He had unbounded confidence in them.[23]

The Chevalier de la Luzerne saw Continental soldiers who were so nearly naked that the French troops laughed at them, but who nevertheless refused to wear coats sent from Spain because they were red like those of the British.[24] Greene witnessed a dauntless spirit among his men that carried them to victory in the Carolinas over almost insurmountable obstacles. Though hundreds of them had tracked the ground with blood on the march to Irwin's Ferry, and the whole army had suffered excessive fatigue, he reported on February 15, 1781, that his troops were in good spirits.[25] A month later he repeated his observation, applying it especially to the Continental troops.[26] Supplies of every kind failed; yet morale was maintained.[27] He felt that neither officers nor men in any army ever showed a better spirit.[28] Only the prospect of lacking salt, when the fear was added to countless other hardships, produced serious discontent.[29] No army was ever in such deplorable condition, he wrote, "and none but ours would keep together under such distressing circumstances."[30]

Washington well summarized this aspect of army morale in the closing months of the war when he called the attention of the Secretary of War to the variety of services performed by American troops. Work such as erecting fortifications, the building of huts and barracks, and the cutting and transporting of wood for all the posts and garrisons was foreign to their proper duty, but had been done without gratuity.[31] The plight and fortitude of his army, he repeated, were without parallel in history.[32] He was convinced that if historians should some day relate the story of American success against incredible obstacles, their work would be called fiction. Readers would not believe that mighty Britain could be baffled by "numbers infinitely less, composed of Men oftentimes half starved . . . in Rags, without pay, and experiencing, at times, every species of distress" that human nature could endure.[33] Devotion to a cause that they held dear is, indeed, the only adequate explanation even now. We are inclined to agree with Washington's conclusion as voiced in his final orders, which were written at Rocky Hill, N. J., in November, 1783, and published in the newspapers: "The unparalleled perseverance of the armies of the United States through almost every possible suffering and discouragement for the space of eight long years was little short of a standing miracle."[34]

# ☆ III ☆

# *Absenteeism and Desertion*

Desertion figures so largely in the problem of morale that it requires special consideration. As in other wars, many soldiers became completely discouraged by hardships and homesickness. There was, moreover, abundant opportunity to escape.[1] The British army, in spite of its comparatively rigid discipline, also suffered considerable desertion, especially among the Hessians.[2] Our previous discussion of the existing hardships, lax discipline, and the use of militia indicates that many important causes of desertion existed in the patriot army to a greater extent than in most armies. Hence it is not surprising to find the problem one of large proportions.[3]

## ABSENTEEISM

Although there is obviously a distinction between absence and desertion, inasmuch as the crime of absence without leave does not imply an intention of remaining away permanently, yet the two are so closely connected that one can best understand both by studying them together. A glance at the army which first gathered informally about Boston reveals a strikingly free and easy code with regard to the soldiers' visiting their homes. A man who wished to leave for a few days might write to a relative or friend asking him to come to camp for a while as his substitute.[4] But even this formality was often dispensed with, and the officers quickly found it necessary to introduce more regularity. Before spring was over, the orderly books began to bristle with directions for calling the roll morning and evening and with warnings that the men must repair to quarters immediately upon tattoo beating.[5] When Washington took command, he proceeded at once to the difficult task of banishing the prevailing laxity and convincing officers and men that unauthorized absence was a serious matter.[6]

The abuse of furloughs was a source of trouble from the first. The number of applications appalled Washington, who roundly scolded both officers and privates for thus "disgracefully desiring to go home" while the campaign was still in its infancy.[7] But despite his best efforts, he was compelled to furlough at least 1500 before the end of November in order to quiet the widespread discontent and enable the men to provide necessities for themselves and their families.[8] Greene actually proposed exchanging the armies in North and South to "cure the itch for going home on furlough" through the simple device of making the distance impracticable, thereby saving the country the needless expense of paying a large body of troops who were absent from camp.[9]

Under such circumstances, adequate discipline of absentees was impossible, even though much of the absence actually amounted to desertion. Washington pardoned a man for confessed absence, refusal to take the oath of allegiance, and threatening to leave the army, because he promised to behave better thereafter.[10] A little later a soldier who had been absent for three months and had disposed of his gun was given a mere fifteen lashes and was compelled to pay for the weapon.[11] Very few were sentenced at all during the first year. Floggings became only slightly more severe before the Articles of War were strengthened in September, 1776.[12] Congress late in 1775 endeavored to provide a system of officers' reports to the Commissary of Musters showing the reasons for absence from muster, so that the commanding officer and Congress might have adequate information.[13] But the orderly books indicate that any improvement that occurred was slow indeed.[14]

Abuse of leave of absence for sickness seems to have been especially glaring. As early as June 12, 1776, Washington forbade such leave of absence except on certification of the Director General of the Hospital, ordered the recall of convalescents then absent, and threatened to treat future offenders as deserters.[15] Yet, many months later, he stated that there were as many absent because of real or pretended illness as though no orders had been issued.[16]

Washington's army continued to suffer from unauthorized absence due to various causes, in spite of repeated orders for frequent roll calls and for careful rounding up of absentees.[17] How ineffective were his best efforts is apparent from orders issued in January, 1780, to the effect that men long absent and unaccounted for should be struck off the rolls, and that the greatest care should be used to collect those "improperly absent" but "still recoverable."[18] The continued abuse of furloughs gives eloquent testimony to the same fact. Officers were so careless that Washington forbade the granting of any furloughs or discharges without his direct consent, especially during periods of crisis.[19] The problem was greatly complicated by the practice of giving furloughs in wholesale fashion to induce the soldiery to reenlist—a policy to which Washington consented only with the greatest reluctance.[20] In the fall of 1777 most of the nine oldest Virginia regiments whose terms expired the following February were thus indulged.

A year later large numbers of other Virginians were allowed four months' leave for the same reason.[21] A similar demand from the North Carolina troops in 1778 gave the Commander-in-Chief such anxiety that he appealed to Congress for advice. Would the men ever return? The precedent, he observed, was bad.[22] But the iniquitous system had to be continued in order to keep an army in the field.[23]

At Boston, Heath was so lenient with regard to absence in the winter of 1777-1778 that the total on leave in some brigades nearly equaled the number present and fit for duty. In April Washington peremptorily ordered him to see that all who had overstayed their furloughs return at once on penalty of being tried as deserters.[24] Alexander McDougall at Peekskill had been so indulgent that the number of absentees in at least one brigade was amazing.[25] Washington endeavored to limit strictly the proportion of men furloughed at any one time, and had his officers publish newspaper notices warning absentees to report or else face desertion charges.[26] He tried to prevent forging of furloughs by requiring (June 8, 1777) that all furloughs be printed,[27] and implored Congress in 1781 to deprive commanding officers of all right to furlough their men.[28] The hospital continued to be a loophole for desertion.[29] As late as February 25, 1783, Washington was compelled to threaten a total cessation of furloughs if there were any further increase in desertion because of their abuse.[30]

The sources reveal similar conditions among the troops not under Washington's immediate command. In 1776 Heath warned his men at Kingsbridge that absence without leave would be treated as desertion[31] and in 1778 he threatened like treatment for exceeding of furloughs and for failure of recruits to join their regiments.[32] His orderly book, however, reveals such leniency in absence cases that the efficacy of his threats may be doubted.[33]

Everywhere there was the same laxity in granting furloughs and observing them; and absence from quarters at night or for days at a time persisted in spite of all efforts of commandants to keep their men together.[34] Penalties for absence appear frequently in the orderly books, but usually amount to mere reprimands, small fines, or a few lashes unless such absence is coupled with other serious offences.[35] Numerous acquittals and pardons, given usually because of extenuating circumstances, also appear.[36] An occasional regiment such as the 2nd Massachusetts chalked up a larger proportion of more severe floggings, but in some of these cases the offender had been tried on charges of desertion and had been convicted of absence, and in still other cases the crime was absence for a year or more.[37] Moreover, even in a strictly disciplined corps a court of inquiry would excuse overstaying of furloughs when excuses seemed good, and such offenders were not prosecuted.[38] Commandants might forbid absence on any pretense, or station a special night guard at a strategic point to detect offenders, but still the problem was unsolved.[39]

It would seem that in the South there was, on the whole, still greater laxity. At Charleston both officers and men assumed that they had the right to leave camp when they pleased. A threat of punishment excepted those "having a very sufficient excuse,"[40] and actual penalties were few and far between.[41] The Supreme Executive Council of Georgia ordered that any militiaman who left camp without permission should forfeit all pay due and be considered an enemy of the State, but there is no indication that the resolution was enforced.[42] Charles Lee found troops at Williamsburg strolling into and out of town at will "without the least ceremony," but he could do nothing more than confirm a sentence of 39 lashes for an offender.[43] At other Virginia towns—such as Suffolk and Springfield, Portsmouth and Smithfield—conditions were similar.[44] Steuben entreated Greene to forbid subordinates' furloughing either officers or men or sending them on command: the country was full of soldiers sent from the army under various pretenses, and the service was suffering greatly. Abuses with regard to discharges were also prevalent.[45] Greene did what he could to correct conditions. One offender was hanged in the sight of the whole army.[46] But he was never able to solve the problem.

Equally troublesome was the universal tendency to straggle from camp or from the line of march in search of excitement and plunder. This unmilitary habit was the root of multiplied disciplinary problems, and contributed greatly to absence and outright desertion. Officers tried to keep their men within a mile of camp, but frequent roll calls, threats, and warnings of the danger involved had little effect.[47] The practice persisted even in the midst of unfriendly Indians lying in wait for scalps.[48]

Before Boston in 1775 the men strolled about the marshes looking for shellfish, heedless of the enemy's artillery.[49] Orders for daily roll call were neglected, and the soldiery continued to straggle from camp after months of effort on the part of Washington to bring some semblance of order into the army.[50] Throughout the war the problem continued in his army without much improvement.[51] At Morristown early in 1780 his rides to and from camp never failed to reveal that the country was "spread over with Soldiers, notwithstanding the pointed orders which have been issued . . . to discountenance a practice which has been found pregnant of desertion, Robbery, and even murders."[52] Three months later, at Short Hills, N. J., he again found stragglers far from camp "on a variety of frivolous pretences and without passes"—a condition which he once more branded as "pernicious" and "subversive of all discipline."[53] At Yorktown in 1781 he urged his officers again to prevent straggling, although it would seem that the prevalence of smallpox and other infection in most of the houses in the vicinity should have constituted a sufficient deterrent.[54]

Before Steuben taught Washington's army to march in compact formation in 1778, it had marched Indian fashion—a system that made discipline on the march almost impossible.[55] Charles Lee had tried in 1776 to improve marching by using a rear guard to prevent straggling, plundering, and other disorders.[56] Washington and other officers had also sought from the first to prevent delay and straggling on the march.[57] But early efforts were ineffectual, and Steuben himself could accomplish little more. Officers and men continued to leave the line of march without much ceremony in order to fill their canteens, to sleep off the effects of drink, or to indulge in mischief.[58]

With absence thus prevalent, conditions favored desertion on a large scale. The average recruit, in fact, had little conception of what desertion or absence without leave involved. To him, leaving the army was something of a right, not a crime.

### THE EXTENT OF DESERTION

The exact amount of desertion in an army is always hard to ascertain.[1] But it is certain that in the Revolutionary army it assumed large proportions, especially among the militia. Irregular troops often rallied with reluctance, and quickly became impatient to return home. Appeals for them to overstay their terms usually met with cold response.[2] The eloquence of a Cicero, as Ebenezer Huntington quaintly expressed it, would no more produce such an effect "than the Niagara falls would the Kindling of a Fire."[3] Lafayette learned in Virginia that "you might as well stop the flood tide as to stop militia whose times are out."[4] Going home when terms were out, to be sure, was not desertion;

but it reveals a significant lack of enthusiasm, and prepares one for the discovery that multitudes failed to wait until their terms expired. In the harvest season they would desert in shoals in order to save their crops.[5] Knowing officers would sometimes dismiss them in great numbers before the men took the law into their own hands.[6] Sumter adopted the plausible expedient of leaving selected persons at home in the busy season to assist their neighbors, but even so he found it impossible to prevent hourly desertions.[7] Usually neither he nor Marion could keep militia in the army for more than two weeks in any season; at times their commands almost evaporated altogether.[8] Winter with its hardships was also sure to take its toll in militia desertion.[9] Any unusual difficulty, in short, would produce an exodus from camp.[10] A circumstance which peculiarly disturbed militia—and that through no fault of theirs—was the horror of captivity which resulted from the difficulty of exchanging militia prisoners and from the British policy of treating many as traitors.[11]

On the frontier the fear of Indian raids produced much militia desertion. The men naturally feared that their homes would be burned and their families scalped or carried off.[12] The partisan raids in the Carolinas had a similar effect. Marion stated that if he left the property and families of the inhabitants exposed to the enemy, his militia would desert almost to a man.[13] Granted that conditions favored a general rallying of militia, it generally proved impossible to keep them in service for any prolonged operation such as a siege.[14] In the Rhode Island campaign of 1778 Washington hoped against hope that putting militia and regulars together in each division in fairly equal numbers would produce better behavior among the State troops.[15] But the commanding officers soon realized the folly of trying to reduce Newport with such a force. When it became apparent that the French fleet could give no immediate help, upward of 3000 militia left in a single day.[16] The entire army was quickly reduced to little more than half its former size.[17]

An adverse turn in the tide of war would produce wholesale desertion of the militia. After Washington's retreat from Long Island, whole companies and regiments left him without ceremony.[18] The demoralization continued for months. The impatience of the militia to go home menaced the very existence of his army.[19] He would gladly have dispensed with them entirely if that had been possible. They "come in you cannot tell how," he declared, "go, you cannot tell when; and act, you cannot tell where; consume your Provisions, exhaust your Stores, and leave you at last in a critical moment."[20] The sorry record continued throughout the war. Vast quantities of public arms and other equipment were taken by such deserters, many of whom had served for scarcely a day.[21] The prolonged uncertainty as to the outcome of the struggle in the South rendered the militia there especially flighty.[22] Those who fled from Camden spread terror everywhere. Attempts to embody more merely kept thousands of them on useless marches to and from camp. Greene likened them to the locusts of Egypt.[23] Hundreds of those collected at Hillsborough after Gates' defeat deserted within a few days.[24] Militia flocked in when they thought Cornwallis would invade Virginia, but disappeared as soon as he marched to Hillsborough.[25] In March, 1781, although upward of 5000 had been in motion during the preceding four weeks, Greene had only about 900 in his army.[26] To an officer of European extraction the whole militia system was amazing. "The devil himself," exclaimed Baron de Kalb, "could not have made a worse arrangement."[27] Without including drafts who never joined the army, it can safely be stated that at least half of the militia enrolled during the war deserted.[28]

Desertion of Continental troops, though not so prevalent as that of militia, was also a serious problem. By 1777 the failure of recruits to join their regiments had become sufficiently pronounced to cause great concern.[29] Washington informed Congress early in 1778 that the drafts from Virginia and North Carolina had dwindled since the preceding fall to almost nothing, and that few could be expected to join his army as long as recruits were brought from their rendezvous at a snail's pace.[30] Steuben's experience with Virginia recruits later in the war was equally disappointing.[31] A Maryland draft in 1780 netted only 381 men who remained in the army for any considerable time. Large numbers deserted immediately after receiving the bounty. Draft evaders in Maryland were known to resist the officers by force, and many apparently made good their escape by leaving the community or the State.[32] Evidently the draft system, as in other wars, produced much desertion during the Revolution.

In 1776 Washington found that surgeons and mates who left camp under the pretext of caring for the sick and wounded had in large part failed to show up.[33] Early next year he attempted to collect vast numbers of convalescents scattered all over the country.[34] Only as a last resort, he advised, should the sick be furloughed, for in general it simply meant so many men lost to the service.[35] Discouragement sometimes produced mass desertion of able-bodied regulars.[36] Commanders in the South often found desertion among their regulars almost as prevalent as among their militia.[37] A return of Colonel Williams' Maryland brigade on August 1, 1781, showed 375 present, 173 absent because of illness, and 268 deserters.[38] Extensive desertion occurred at Valley Forge in 1777-1778 because of the rigors of the winter and the comfortable situation of the British in Philadelphia. The total number of deserters during that period must have been well over 2000.[39]

Actual statistics on desertion are meager. Muster rolls usually omit such data. Even when deserters are designated, in many cases only those who made good their escape are included. The lists of Massachusetts soldiers, which are among the most complete rolls available, mark about one man in fifty as a deserter. But it appears that many men are listed several times, and that many were volunteers without definite terms or militia called out for a few days only. These lists, moreover, fail to designate men as "missing," "unaccounted for," or "struck off," although rolls of other States show large numbers in such categories.[40] These facts, along with evidence already noted of wholesale desertion among Bay State militia, compel one to question the accuracy of the data.

The Maryland rolls omit any data on discharges for large numbers of men, and designate many as missing. About a fifth of the total are marked "deserted." If there were many deserters among the doubtful cases, and it stands to reason that there were, the proportion of deserters must have been from a fourth to a third of the privates.[41]

But the most complete data on desertion appear in the New York rolls. Of the seven Continental regiments listed, the first has 17 out of 150 officers marked "deserted" and several more "omitted." The proportion of officers who deserted runs higher in most of the other regiments. Of about 900 officers in the seven regiments, at least 135, or over 15%, deserted. At least a third of all the privates deserted. In at least one regiment over a fourth of the officers and nearly half of the privates were deserters.[42]

It would seem that at least a third of the regular troops enlisted in the Revolutionary army became deserters.

## THE CAUSES OF DESERTION

Numerous motives prompted desertion. Rarely did one factor alone influence the offender. By far the most important causes, it will appear, were the factors discussed in the first chapter, such as quality of troops, hardships, inadequate pay, and the bounty system. The recruiting of disaffected men, especially the foreign-born, prisoners of war, and deserters from the enemy, was a contributing factor of some importance. The effect of the draft system has already been noticed.[1] Unworthy officers sometimes incited their men to desert.[2] Irregular discharges were a source of trouble.[3] Numbers of men of Loyalist inclinations, especially those of foreign extraction, were influenced by Sir William Howe's proclamation offering pardons and bounties to any patriots who joined him.[4] Most of the deserters from Valley Forge were foreign-born.[5] It was generally assumed that "Old Countrymen," as Europeans were called, easily went to the enemy.[6]

The enlisting of deserters and prisoners from the British army caused constant trouble. Such recruits demoralized the other troops and deserted upon the least excuse. Washington warned especially against enrolling deserting British officers, whom he believed to be of base character without exception.[7] The southern States' policy of condemning militia delinquents and other undesirables to service in the Continental line also bore bitter fruit.[8] So important was the Loyalist element in the southern army that flagrant cases of desertion often prompted the suspicion that British emissaries were at work.[9] Recruiting standards which grew out of seven years of war reflect significant disillusionment over the use of unreliable men. In 1782 Lieut. Col. Jeremiah Olney gave notice in his advertising for recruits in Providence that he would receive only white men who had served three years or more in the Continental army, or who were married and had lived in the State at least three years.[10]

Homesickness and aversion to service in another State, especially a dread on the part of northern men of service in the South, is also worth considering. Schuyler found that homesickness in the northern army became a major ailment in mid-October and increased in severity as the winter advanced.[11] Officers in Middle and Southern Departments made similar observations.[12] Washington detached troops for service in the South with the greatest reluctance, for he knew that a large part of them would fall off during the long march through sickness and desertion.[13] In 1781 he stated that, from first to last, a third and possibly half of the men sent to the South were lost in this way.[14] Lafayette found that some of his best troops preferred 100 lashes to such a journey.[15]

A more general cause of desertion was the bounty system. Even before the plan went into operation, Washington was compelled to denounce paid agents who were discovered seducing men to leave their regiments and re-enlist in others.[16] With the appearance of State and Congressional bounties, "bounty jumping" quickly became such a menace that he threatened death for the guilty.[17] "The practice has prevailed to a great and scandalous degree," he wrote in May, 1777.[18] A year later he emphasized the discontent which huge State bounties produced among the veterans, and declared that most of the desertion at that time, especially in those cases when the culprits did not go to the enemy, was due to the bounty system.[19] The practice of deserting in order to reenlist was widespread during most of the war.[20] Virginia's policy of short enlistments and high bounties made the traffic there quite flagrant during the later years.[21] Peter Muhlenberg reported one offender (July 9, 1782) who was perhaps too notorious to be typical, but nevertheless reveals something of the general character of his class. He was one of several former deserters who had been sent to the army as substitutes and who had recently enticed eleven others to desert. The worst of the lot, by his own confession he had deserted no less than four times, had stolen a horse, forged a discharge and a pass in Muhlenberg's name, and joined the British during the last campaign.[22]

After 1777 a great deal of desertion was traceable to the deficiencies in wages. Washington thought that Howe's proclamation in 1777 would have had no effect if his men had been promptly paid.[23] Failure to pay bounties that had been promised caused great discontent.[24] Payment of arrears in pay and improvement in the provisioning of the army had a noticeable effect in reducing desertion.[25] The financial stringency after 1778 was disastrous in its effects. Extraordinary Congressional and State bounties could not cope with the increasing desertion.[26] By the spring of 1781, from 100 to 200 men from Washington's army were going to the enemy every month.[27] A year later, returns revealed that the situation was still more acute.[28] In the South, men served through difficult campaigns with no pay and little prospect of any, until their staying in the army seemed a miracle. The almost total lack of money during Greene's service there contributed largely to the extensive desertion that prevailed.[29]

Other hardships constituted a further cause of desertion. Smallpox and other diseases greatly aggravated the evil, especially in the northern army.[30] Lack of clothing was even more demoralizing. Wayne was confident that not one in twenty of the desertions in the Pennsylvania line during the winter 1777-1778 would have occurred if the men had been adequately clothed.[31] The very existence of the southern forces was threatened by a chronic lack of clothing.[32] Desertion from the cavalry serving in the Carolinas in 1780 became so general because of near nakedness that two corps had to be sent back to Virginia.[33]

When to nakedness is added hunger, the stage setting for the forlorn drama of desertion is complete. There were cases when desertion was actually the alternative to starvation.[34] Scarcity of flour sometimes caused the desertion of whole corps that had previously behaved well.[35] The increase in desertion when food ran short always made lack of provisions a matter of vital concern to Washington. Prolonged periods of deprivation such as those in 1780 produced general demoralization. "Complaints and murmuring, a relaxation of discipline, marauding, robbery and desertion are the consequences," he declared at a time when there was no meat for days, "and indeed it is to be wondered at that they have not prevailed to a much greater extent."[36]

There are multiplied instances of such an accumulation of hardships of various kinds that army life for many became unendurable. The untold suffering during Arnold's expedition to Quebec resulted in the defection of almost a third of his force at a stroke.[37] Colonel Scammell, appalled by the suffering at Valley Forge, almost repented that he had accepted the office of Adjutant General: the complaints of officers and men were heartrending. It appeared that the army must dissolve.[38] In Washington's opinion, an attack by Sir Henry Clinton upon the army at Morristown during the severe winter of 1779-1780 would have precipitated a disaster. Acute suffering for want of food and clothing during those months produced desertion only less serious than that at Valley Forge.[39] In 1782 the lack of every necessity almost dissolved the patriot forces throughout the country.[40]

It is apparent that, while numerous factors must be considered, yet the use of many unfit men and the hardships suffered by the army constituted by far the most important causes of desertion during the Revolution.

### THE PREVENTION OF DESERTION

All the efforts to maintain morale which are discussed in the last chapter tended to prevent desertion. But there were other devices directed specifically to that end which claim attention at this point.

Obviously the responsibility for preventing desertion rested largely upon the officers. Unfortunately they did not always discharge the obligation. Indeed, they sometimes recruited worthless men who quickly deserted, absentees from the army, or British deserters.[1] Many failed to enter upon company books full data for each recruit, including place of residence, although such negligence made the recovery of deserters difficult.[2] In some cases they promised recruits that they would not be sent out of their home districts, and thus laid the basis for desertion when the men were undeceived.[3] The whole recruiting process, in fact, opened many a loophole for desertion. Washington urged that officers should advance as little of the bounty as possible until the company was complete, and above all should get the men to the army as quickly as possible.[4] But officers were inclined to take their time, and large numbers of recruits continued to escape before they reached the army.[5]

Washington was also obliged to convince both civil and military officers that captivity at the hands of the enemy could not entitle those who escaped to a discharge from the army. Many soldiers considered that their refusal while prisoners to engage in British service somehow merited such a reward, and some proceeded to act on the assumption; but it seems that he was able to forestall any general desertion of this type.[6]

The frequent roll calls on which Washington and other careful officers insisted were calculated to prevent desertion as well as straggling or absence without leave. The neglect of such precautions by many officers was one of the reasons Washington assigned for the extensive desertion from his army.[7] He was also convinced of the obvious necessity of giving idle men something to do. Troops off duty, he stated, should be maneuvered and disciplined daily. The policy, to use his own words, would "prevent Idleness and Dissipation, which are too frequently and fatally attended by Desertion."[8]

Equally obvious to a modern observer was the wisdom of refusing pay to absentees, of changing the countersign in case of desertion from the outposts, and of arresting on charges of desertion soldiers found at an improper distance from camp or engaged in activities that indicated an intention to desert; but the manner in which such procedures were mentioned in Washington's orders reveals a decided tendency on the part of subordinates to neglect them.[9] Steuben detected many of the weaknesses in the system. Careless officers, he pointed out, allowed men to absent themselves without reason and neglected to bring back convalescents. Hospital doctors gave furloughs and discharges unnecessarily. Printed forms for discharges, he thought, would prevent counterfeiting. Inferior officers should not grant discharges. Southern men who went home should be required to present discharges or furloughs to county lieutenants or else be treated as deserters. County lieutenants should round up deserters and ferret out discharges given without cause.[10]

Washington actually adopted some policies similar to these,[11] and recommended to Congress the general use of printed certificates which should be presented to the nearest magistrate within ten days of the soldiers' return home.[12] But there is no evidence that the plan urged by Steuben was generally used. Washington also recommended the posting of a chain of sentries around each encampment during a march, the stationing of details at army hospitals and at ferries, and the policy of hourly roll calls by day and equally frequent visitation of quarters by night in case desertion should begin.[13] Had all officers been equally diligent, his efforts might have been fruitful.[14]

Seduction to desertion, and harboring of deserters, were not unknown in the army.[15] These offenses, however, were more often the work of civilians or prisoners of war. Heath was frequently compelled to deal with this problem. In 1776 he warned his men at Kingsbridge that disaffected persons were trying to discourage the soldiery by harping on the hopeless outlook for the patriot cause, and ordered that the offenders be arrested.[16] At Boston, while responsible for the Saratoga prisoners, he made strenuous but apparently ineffectual efforts to prevent contacts between the prisoners and his men.[17] Finally, at the Highlands in 1782, he endeavored to keep Tories and prisoners of war who were in the provost at West Point and Fishkill from going out on fatigue duty or otherwise mixing with the troops.[18]

There were several cases of Tory inhabitants' being tried by court martial and sentenced for enticing soldiers to desert to the enemy. Such Loyalist offenders were treated as spies, and therefore received the death penalty.[19] The danger of a clash with State authorities, however, caused army officers to hesitate at times over such drastic procedure, and they left many cases in the hands of State governors.[20] Washington issued orders at Valley Forge to stop Philadelphia women from coming into camp under pretense of visiting their friends in the army and of returning with articles needed by soldiers' families. Their real purpose, he said, was to entice the men to desert.[21] In April he ordered Smallwood to send the Delaware battalion to camp at once and to forward all new recruits as fast as they were raised. The Delaware Loyalists were not only carrying on illicit trade with the enemy but were constantly seducing recruits to desert and then harboring them or sending them off to the enemy.[22] Next spring, while the army was at Middlebrook, such Loyalist activity became so pronounced that he gave strict orders to watch the company the soldiers kept, and informed Governor Livingston that he planned to withdraw the Monmouth detachment as well as that at Elizabethtown, partly on account of the active enemy agents in that region. He also implored the governor to deal drastically with two offenders under arrest as examples to the Tories.[23]

Effective prevention of desertion, however, must depend on efficient apprehension and punishment of offenders who made their escape. Hence the best officers gave serious attention from the first to these aspects of the problem. Not long after his arrival at Cambridge in 1775, Washington revealed his full realization of the situation. Not only were absentees appallingly numerous, he declared, but most of them were at home—"infamous Deserters and Defrauders of the Public."[24] With all that could be done through the use of patrols and scouting parties to intercept fugitives, it was impossible throughout the war to prevent the great majority of deserters from making good their escape.[25] The sources indicate thousands who left the army, but a mere handful who were caught.[26]

Hence great dependence was placed on recruiting officers, who were expected to round up deserters as well as to enlist new men. The work was considered a regular part of the recruiting business, whether carried on by military or civil officers.[27] The minor part played by civilians in recruiting during the Revolution, however, threw most of the burden upon army officers, and they were constantly exhorted to diligence in the matter.[28] The degree of success attained is difficult to ascertain, but it is certain that recruiting officers handled considerable numbers of deserters.[29] Whatever the method used, efforts were always severely handicapped by the widespread tendency of civilians to harbor fugitives. The Loyalist element in the population was large, and the people as a whole were not military minded. Sentimental considerations only too easily eclipsed their feeble loyalty to the army.[30] Officers constantly appealed for vigorous measures. As early as June 19, 1775, Stark asked the New Hampshire Committee of Safety to recommend that towns and parishes arrest and return all men of the New Hampshire line stationed at Medford who should be found away from the army without furloughs.[31] On August 7, Washington called upon the Massachusetts legislature to co-operate with him in dealing with large numbers of deserters who were at their homes, some of them engaged in regular civilian employments, but the response was disappointing.[32] Charles Lee encountered the problem in Virginia, where recruits from the back country, especially the Irish, deserted in such numbers that he suggested enjoining the county committees to seize soldiers who could not produce discharges or passes.[33] The complacence of State authorities is indicated by Connecticut's wage settlements with men who had deserted. The petitioners' plea was that they had left camp because they thought their terms were up.[34]

By 1777 the situation had become alarming indeed. Washington now implored Congress to exert pressure on the States for vigorous action. He declared that, unless people could be forced to give information about deserters in their home communities, he would be "obliged to detach one half of the Army to bring back the other."[35] He feared that the widespread harboring of deserters would result in the evaporation of the new army as fast as it was recruited, and in a vigorous letter to the States he insisted on adequate measures.[36] That he strongly preferred Congressional to State action, however, is indicated by a letter some three weeks later to Reed, expressing apprehension lest the States "have some newfangled, or inadequate schemes of their own" before Congress perfected a plan.[37]

The slowness of the States was particularly trying in view of a recommendation that Congress had made as early as November 4, 1775, to the effect that fines of from $30 to $50 be inflicted on persons harboring deserters.[38] Next year Congress brought special pressure upon Pennsylvania. In view of the extensive desertion from three of its battalions, the State was urged to use the German battalion if necessary to return the culprits to camp, and was exhorted also to allay discontent by supplying clothing and blankets.[39] But State authorities were loath to assume responsibility.

Meanwhile Congress offered to pay $5 and expenses to any one bringing a deserter back to the army, the reward to be deducted from the offender's wages.[40] Washington's letter in 1777 apparently had its influence, for in February Congress appointed a committee to investigate, and, after some hesitation, called upon State committees of observation to round up deserters and send them to the nearest Continental officer, and offered a reward of $8 and expenses to any person delivering an offender. The resolution, along with pertinent selections from the Articles of War, was published in the papers and was ordered printed also on handbills for circulation among army officers.[41] The reward was increased next month to $10, and was soon offered to non-commissioned officers and privates as well as to civilians.[42] At the same time, drastic laws against harboring deserters and receiving their public property were recommended to the legislatures.[43] In 1779, State governors were authorized to allow £30 reward and 3s. per mile for transportation, with Congress footing the bill, and again the legislatures were asked to take action. Deserters should be delivered at once to the army when arrested, Congress urged, because of the expense of keeping them in prison. An order from a justice of the peace was sufficient authority for taking such offenders from jail if the army officers were at a distance from the seat of government. If there were no military officers in the State, the militia should take the criminals from places of rendezvous to the army.[44]

These measures had some effect,[45] but there is no evidence that they presented anything like a satisfactory solution. Local co-operation was too often lacking.[46] State legislation was tardy and often lacked thoroughness. Such laws endeavored to place responsibility upon local officials for apprehending deserters, and urged the populace to co-operate. Most States offered rewards for securing deserters and imposed small penalties for concealing them.[47] Attempts were made to strengthen the system as the war progressed, but the legislators themselves only too often were obliged to confess that the laws were ineffective.[48]

Numerous advertisements of deserters appeared in the newspapers, especially during the years 1776-1781.[49] These were usually inserted by army officers, and offered small rewards and payment of expenses for apprehension of fugitives.[50] Muhlenberg offered $1,000 and expenses for a sergeant, corporal, and six men who deserted in 1780 (taking their arms with them), but this reward was much higher than the average.[51] The notices remind one strongly of advertisements for runaway slaves which appeared in the same papers; however, the rewards offered for apprehending the deserters were decidedly smaller.[52] Descriptions of fugitives were sometimes minute.[53] Captured offenders were ordinarily to be delivered to their officers, but occasionally an advertiser was content with having them brought to a jail.[54] Sometimes a jailer was obliged to advertise a deserter who had escaped from his custody.[55] Such advertisements were fairly well distributed over the six years during which the great bulk of them appeared, but individual publications show much variation according to local conditions.[56]

There are many expense accounts and other bits of evidence to show that some deserters were brought in by various means from late 1775 to 1781, with both soldiers and civilians participating in the process.[57] But the constant efforts to improve the system, the attempts of army officers to get lists of deserters of long standing whose whereabouts was well known, and the many offers of pardon to induce deserters to surrender, indicate that the laws could not be well enforced.[58] Richard Dallam asked Governor Thomas Lee of Maryland for permission to make terms with deserters in Hartford County whom he could not secure. They were applying to him for liberty to secure substitutes. He had been offered 100 bushels of wheat to get a discharge for one fellow. The striking of advantageous bargains, he suggested, would net the State something, whereas if the scoundrels were returned to the army they would be of little use![59]

Considerable sections of the country, as during the Civil War, became recognized hideouts for deserters. Inaccessibility and Loyalist influence rendered such districts as the lower counties of New Jersey excellent places of refuge. Henry Lee found no effort on the part of State authorities to aid him to collect fugitives about Dover, but encountered plenty of influential men who harbored the guilty. If Washington could influence the legislature to authorize the arrest of such Tories in high places, he said, "great advantages might accrue to the army."[60] S. H. Parsons found difficulty at Redding, where few people would give him aid, but many concealed his deserters and positively refused to deliver them up.[61]

The South offered many such places of security. Richard Henry Lee described three "atrocious piratical Villains" from the Virginia line in 1780 who had "armed themselves and attempted to plunder and raise a Crew of Desperadoes to ravage both sides of the river Patowmack," and the Maryland council made an effort to apprehend them. Over a year later the report came back from Leonardtown that one of the desperate trio had been taken, but the other two were still bidding defiance to the authorities at the point of the gun.[62] Hundreds of such lawless deserters lurked in parts of Virginia such as Hampshire, Montgomery, and Washington Counties, spreading disaffection and engaging on occasion in armed riots. Army officers could get no co-operation from the State in their efforts to deal with the situation.[63] Cavalry deserters from Greene's army in 1783 actually browbeat the Virginia legislature into paying instead of prosecuting them.[64]

Large numbers of deserters found refuge also in the Carolinas. In North Carolina they were so numerous by the end of 1776 that Governor Richard Caswell, on request of the Council of State, issued a proclamation requiring them to return, warning people against harboring them, and urging civil and military officers to use all diligence in apprehending them.[65] Deserters from the regular army stationed in Georgia found refuge in the Carolinas as well as in Virginia.[66] The willingness with which deserters in the South were received and forgiven by their neighbors had a demoralizing effect on the army. Soldiers deserted on the presumption that they too would be forgiven.[67] There is evidence that the number of fugitives increased with the progress of the war.[68]

Quite naturally the frontier throughout the country made a refuge for swarms of deserters whom the arm of the law could not reach. The county lieutenants at Salisbury, N. C., declared in

1780 that the jails would not hold the fugitives who were being entertained in the county.[69] A new frontier settlement in Tennessee or Kentucky was sure to form a dangerous center for outlaws from every State and deserters from both British and American armies.[70] In Ulster and Orange Counties in New York a band of Indians, joined by Tories and deserters and supplied with provisions by Loyalist inhabitants, operated from points on the Delaware to terrorize the countryside.[71] George Rogers Clark wrote from Louisville that his recruiting for the Kaskaskia-Vincennes expedition had gone forward satisfactorily until many leading men in the West "through a spirit of obstinacy . . . did every thing in their power to stop the Men that had Enlisted, and set the whole Fronteers [sic] in an uproar," openly harboring deserters from his army.[72] He himself extended protection for a time to deserters from the Spanish forces, and Governor Bernardo de Galvez gave refuge to American deserters even after Clark had reversed his policy in 1779.[73] Western Pennsylvania sheltered fugitives from both East and West, so that Edward Hand wrote from Ft. Pitt in 1778: "I believe the Devil has possessed both Country People and Garrison."[74]

The certainty that new settlements would become retreats for deserters led to severe criticism of State land policies. President Reed told Washington bitterly that Pennsylvania would have kept more of her soldiers enlisted for the war "if the Land-Office in Virginia had not afforded both an asylum and a temptation for desertion." In Kentucky and surrounding regions, he said, many deserters lived without fear of military service or taxation, enjoying "a sort of savage freedom."[75] A group of officers who tried to defeat a bill pending in the Pennsylvania House for the sale of western lands (1781) pointed out not only that the land had been promised them as a reward for their services but also that "a new

Settlement invariably proves to be a Secure assylum [sic] for Deserters from every Quarter."[76]

By the end of the war Vermont had become the home of many hundreds of deserters from Washington's army. Along with a host of persons who sought a haven from taxation and the restraints of the law, they had acquired land there, and were prepared to fight to a finish any attempt to coerce them.[77]

It is evident that apprehension of deserters during the Revolution was never effective enough to constitute any considerable deterrent to desertion. Laws on the subject were never adequate or well enforced. Popular sympathy for the fugitive, weak government, and frontier lawlessness were effective obstacles. The army was not merely left to its own resources in dealing with the problem; it was positively obstructed on every side. "There have been many instances," Washington ruefully observed, "where Deserters which have been apprehended by Officers, have been rescued by the People, and but very few where the Officers have received their aid and support."[78]

It was difficult to mete out adequate discipline even to those deserters who were caught. The first Articles of War permitted only a light flogging or similarly inadequate penalty for so serious a crime. The death penalty was possible for desertion to the enemy after the amendments of November 7, 1775, but it was permitted for all types of desertion only under the new Articles of 1776.[79] Hence, during the first year and a half, offenders were let off with such penalties as reprimands, small fines (usually the expenses of apprehension), refunding of the bounty in cases of reenlistment, dismissal from the army, extra fatigue duty, a few days' confinement, or a flogging of 39 lashes or less. The death penalty in this period was extremely rare.[80] Even so, pardons were frequent. The deserters from an entire corps might be promised leniency if they would return within a few days.[81] Schuyler pardoned thirteen at once out of pure exasperation over the inadequacy of their penalties—fines of one month's wages.[82]

Confronted by a military code that was too lenient to command respect and handicapped by a set of officers that could not be trusted to enforce what little law there was, Washington found 30 or 40 men deserting in batches, but was unable to persuade them to remain.[83] Even when the revised code made 100 lashes or death possible, improvement was hardly perceptible. Officers failed in many cases to have deserters arrested and tried or even reported to headquarters.[84] The number of officers cashiered and otherwise disciplined for actually encouraging desertion is evidence of the obstacles encountered.[85]

It required more than an officious resolution of Congress urging severity under the new code (November 7, 1776) to solve the problem.[86] A better gradation of penalties would have been more to the point. A hundred lashes on the one hand, especially as they were sometimes jokingly given, or death on the other hand, placed the conscientious officer in a dilemma. Robert Howe disapproved a penalty of 100 lashes in one case as "very inadequate:" the criminal had deserted several times with the intention of joining the enemy, and 100 lashes recently inflicted had done no good; indeed, the "puny punishment" was so trifling that he ordered the offender released to join his regiment.[87] And yet the death sentence was so drastic that its use by a court merely invited a general to issue a pardon. Knox once wrote to Washington that one George Baker, sentenced to die, was a scoundrel, who had deserted from the British, had gone back to them, and then had returned; "were the War to continue ten Years longer he would be for changing sides once or twice a year." Still, Knox recommended a pardon![88]

John Laurance, Judge Advocate, sagely observed that too many death penalties would lessen the deterrent effect of executions and deprive the army of too many men, but that the limit of 100 lashes for floggings was a mistake. Most men considered such a whipping trivial.[89] Washington himself disliked the death penalty and used it only as a last resort when he thought the deterrent effect would be greatest.[90] He was alarmed by Henry Lee's suggestion that deserters be executed at once and that their heads should then be sent to the light horse as grisly reminders to discourage desertion. An execution in an occasional flagrant case might do, he hastened to advise, but by no means anything more.[91] He had a way of threatening offenders with the extreme penalty, and then of pardoning most of them at the last minute.[92] He could be adamant against petitions for the pardoning of a man whom he was determined to execute as an example, but was known to yield to the entreaties of a "poor old Man" in behalf of a son.[93]

It cannot be assumed that more rigid discipline would have solved the problem of desertion in the American army. The British not infrequently administered 1,000 lashes, and did not scruple to use the death sentence; yet their army suffered much from desertion.[94] Certainty of detection would have meant more than mere severity.[95] But American officers were unable either to apprehend offenders or to punish them adequately, and so could present little deterrent whatsoever. A flogging of 100 lashes or less and payment of the expenses of apprehension and of a bounty wrongfully received constituted the usual penalty from late 1776 to 1783.[96] The death sentence was much more common than under the first Articles of War, but in most of these cases pardons were given. Out of about 225 men receiving the death penalty whose cases have come to our attention, only some 40 can be stated with certainty to have died the death.[97] However, the fact that no pardons or reprieves are on record for many others, and that the sources are often of fragmentary nature, suggests that there were considerably more executions than that. The pity of it is that even such examples largely failed of their purpose. Three men deserted from Jethro Sumner's force in North Carolina the very evening of the day when a deserter was shot, and others followed suit during the days following.[98] Desertion was large and continuous in Washington's army while the death penalty was most used.[99] When the vast majority who attempted to escape succeeded, discontented men were always ready to take the risk.

### LENIENCY TOWARD DESERTION

There was, furthermore, a good chance that the penalty would be trifling even if a man was caught. Out of about 1,000 penalties for desertion after October, 1776, that have come to our attention, at least 70% were floggings, and of these whippings almost 30% were less than 100 lashes. To the end of the war, penalties of 20 or 25 lashes, fines of a few dollars, imprisonment, and dismissal from the service were not infrequent for this serious offense.[1] Some of the miscellaneous penalties, to be sure, were somewhat more drastic than these.[2] Sentences could also be cumulative.[3] Several non-commissioned officers were reduced, usually in addition to some other penalty.[4] But on the whole the deserter faced good chances of lenient treatment.

Not only did the average deserter count on a mild penalty, but he also had a fair chance of pardon. On various grounds, such as the youthfulness of the offender, ignorance, insanity, or other extenuating circumstances, and especially because of the intercession of deserters' friends, generals remitted many of the lesser penalties[5] and, as already indicated, a large proportion of the death sentences.[6] Washington at times pardoned from ten to twenty or more at once. Heath pardoned 26, and Sullivan 29, at a single stroke.[7]

A significant comment on the general attitude toward desertion and on the failure to apprehend a large proportion of offenders is the frequent use of proclamations of pardon. The need of men for the army outweighed the demand for adequate discipline. Both Congress and the States, as well as army officers, used this device to induce men to return. Such proclamations offered pardon to deserters who would give themselves up within a given time, and threatened drastic treatment of all who refused to comply. They were more or less widely published in the newspapers and occasionally in handbills.[8] Washington at times permitted recruiting officers to extend pardons to deserters in limited areas.[9] On four occasions he issued proclamations covering the entire army. The first appeared April 6, 1777, and set May 15 as the time limit.[10] In October of the same year, acting on an order from Congress, he issued another covering the period to January 1, 1778.[11] The third, issued March 10, 1779, set the limit at May 1; but the period of grace proved too short, and was extended to July 1, thus covering altogether over three and a half months.[12] The last one was issued early in 1782 in the hope of dissolving the "New Corps" organized by the British out of men formerly in the patriot army, and applied only to deserters in enemy service.[13]

The results of these proclamations were disappointing. Only an occasional deserter came in to claim the proffered pardon.[14] Men skulking in out-of-the-way places generally remained ignorant of the offers, and those whom the newspapers reached preferred running the small risk of apprehension to serving again in the army.[15] Those who came in might be notorious criminals, intent on further mischief, and better executed than pardoned.[16] The effect of the first proclamation which Washington issued was so small that he placed little confidence in the second one.[17] In 1780 he informed the Board of War that he had never found such offers of pardon to be "attended with any substantial advantages," and declared that a proclamation which had been requested for the Virginia line would actually encourage future desertion.[18] Men were too likely to presume on such mercy. "The Soldier goes off or remains at home after a furlough, and looks for a proclamation as a thing of course."[19] He did not, however, give up all hope. As late as 1782 he encouraged the States to issue proclamations resembling his own of that year for deserters in British service.[20]

Enough has been said to indicate that the laxity of army officers, misplaced popular sympathies, ineffective military discipline, and the safe refuges offered by a new country combined to render the prevention of desertion a well-nigh hopeless matter. Dire threats of hanging or of shooting on the spot any man attempting to desert, or of future enforcement of army law without mercy, were merely a bluff.[21] Detection was too difficult, penalties were too light, and pardons too frequent to present any real deterrent.

## ☆ IV ☆

# *The Maintenance of Morale*

In the eighteenth century the terms "morale" and "propaganda" had not yet come into use. The general organization of all branches of military service was far less scientific than it is today. Hence, efforts to maintain morale in that day are likely to appear to us haphazard and inadequate. And yet the problem was so critical to Revolutionary leaders that circumstances made it imperative to devise various ways and means of solving it.

### REWARDS, RECREATION, AND REGALIA

Congress and the States gave occasional rewards to soldiers in acknowledgment of outstanding services. Gifts of money, trophies of battle, ornamental swords, and medals were thus employed.[1] Popular officers like Washington and Greene received generous donations of land, horses, and other articles.[2] Some monuments were voted, although few were actually erected, to fallen officers of distinction.[3] But flagrant neglect of the army unfortunately offset the effect of these outbursts of generosity. Hamilton truthfully remarked: "In what Congress have at any time done for the army, they have commonly been too late."[4] His statement would apply equally well to the States.[5]

The value of recreation as an aid to morale was little realized. There was a theatrical performance (April 15, 1778) in the bakehouse at Valley Forge,[6] the officers at Morristown in 1780 subscribed funds for a dancing assembly,[7] and a chaplain was responsible for erecting an auditorium at Newburgh in 1783 for religious services and other assemblages.[8] But recreation in the army was largely unorganized and incidental. The prohibition of gambling put a taboo on billiards, cards, and even the informal "pitch penny" of which the men were fond.[9] Officers attempted to prohibit Sunday diversions, and to restrict vigorous sports like swimming or playing at fives in the summer.[10] Washington exhorted his officers to spend their leisure time studying military tactics and training their men.[11]

Numerous celebrations supplied both recreation and a stimulus to patriotism. Holidays were observed with much hilarity. Patriotic anniversaries in large numbers served to raise the patriot's spirits to the boiling point. By relaxation of fatigue duty, pardons to men under confinement, barbecues, banquets, fireworks, and fervid oratory, such observances supplied a most valuable stimulus to morale.[12]

Various flags were used before the grand raising of the Continental flag at Cambridge in January, 1776.[13] The Stars and Stripes were officially promulgated on September 3, 1777, and probably first appeared in battle at Brandywine eight days later.[14] This flag was used thereafter, along with standards, regimental colors, and division colors.[15] Washington considered the use of flags essential to both discipline and morale.[16]

Music in the army was not much developed beyond fife and drum corps. However, a few other instruments were in use, and there was a superintendent of music from 1778 to 1783.[17] Music was very effective in recruiting.[18] The men set much store by it, and there is no doubt as to its importance for morale. Washington was convinced that it prevented desertion.[19] Of possibly greater importance than instrumental music were army songs, a large number of which were produced during the Revolution.[20]

Both officers and men were fond of uniforms, and Washington realized their importance.[21] But lack of planning and of finance prevented the consistent use of recognized types, and the war ended with the army wearing "a thousand different colours."[22] To supply the deficiency, many distinguishing devices were used, especially hunting shirts, hat decorations, and regimental buttons.[23] William Irvine deplored the lack of distinction in dress between privates and non-commissioned officers. He thought that the latter would be more pleased by appropriate uniforms than by an increase in pay.[24] Wayne declared that he had rather risk his life and reputation leading well-dressed men to an attack with only bayonets and one round of ammunition than to lead them with sixty rounds and their usual nondescript clothes.[25]

Perhaps the nearest approach to a systematic use of regalia was Washington's creation of two orders of military merit; a Badge of Merit to reward length of service, and the Purple Heart to honor distinguished service. Unfortunately this action came too late (August 7, 1782) to be really effective during the war.[26]

## PROPAGANDA

With such a paucity of organization and equipment for the maintenance of morale, propaganda and personal influence assumed great importance. Propaganda was often effective in spite of the inadequate facilities for its dissemination. The Revolution was something of a crusade, preached by pulpit and platform and press. The celebrations discussed in the previous section owed much of their effectiveness to the orator. Chaplains and pamphleteers found audience in the army. Officers were important propagandists.[1]

In an age of strong religious faith on the part of the masses, the clergy were far more important as propagandists than they are today.[2] Ministers of the gospel were largely advocates of the Revolution, and their fiery political sermons had a wide influence.[3] Unfortunately there was never adequate provision for chaplains. Able men were therefore hard to procure, and there were too few of any caliber to meet pressing army needs.[4] This niggardliness caused much complaint among both officers and men, who appreciated the ministrations of able clergymen.[5] Religious services were held regularly among most of the troops, and attendance was required.[6] There was considerable neglect of such meetings.[7] Yet the best officers, including Washington, emphasized the value of good chaplains for promoting happiness and good morals among the soldiers, supporting discipline, and inspiring the army to intelligent and fervent patriotism.[8] Their visitation of the sick and wounded was especially appreciated.[9] Some took up arms on occasion and fought side by side with the men.[10]

A few able ministers in the army were notably successful in bolstering morale. Such were Peter Muhlenberg, famed as the "fighting parson," and fiery John Cleaveland, who was said to have preached his whole parish into the army and then to have gone himself.[11] Rev. John Murray of Maine was so successful in preaching men into the service and in carrying messages for the army that the British offered £500 for his arrest. Rev. Thomas Allen of Pittsfield persuaded a whole corps of discontented men in Lincoln's army to remain in service.[12] There were, of course, chaplains of different spirit, who were absent when most needed.[13] But on the whole it appears that chaplains were a strong bulwark of army morale.

A second important agency of propaganda was the press.[14] An obvious limitation on the use of this medium was the difficulty of communication, with resulting delay and uncertainty of news.[15] Rumors were often more numerous than facts.[16] In 1781, for example, the northern army was on tenterhooks much of the time for lack of authentic reports from the South, while Greene on his part was in the dark as to the events in the North.[17] Thus careful men developed a wholesome skepticism with regard to unofficial reports.[18] Newspapers sometimes neglected or perverted important news.[19] Congress aggravated the problem by frequent neglect to publish information promptly, although Washington urged better publicity.[20]

The papers, however, contained many news items of value, and were eagerly sought by army officers. There is no evidence that they circulated widely among the rank and file. In fact, the opposite was probably the case, inasmuch as officers commonly exchanged the precious copies that came to hand as though they were rare possessions.[21] Handbills also circulated occasionally in the army, some of them unreliable but many possessing real merit and receiving official sanction. Accounts of victories formed the usual contents of these broadsides. Washington considered them valuable in bolstering morale.[22] Apparently only the officers were supplied with copies, and they read them to their men.[23] Pamphlets and books appeared in camp in very limited numbers, but included some propagandist publications such as *Common Sense*, the Declaration of Independence, and *The Crisis*, which had great influence on the army.[24]

Officers soon realized the need for a definite publicity organization. Washington urged upon Congress (1777) the advisability of a small traveling press at his headquarters "to give speedy and exact information of any Military transactions that take place with proper comments upon them," and thus to offset the falsehoods spread by both friend and foe, to furnish a recognized medium of official war reports, and to maintain popular morale. An able man to manage such a press and spend his entire time writing for it, he urged, would "render it singularly beneficial."[25] Congress had paid Fleury Mesplet $200 and expenses in 1776 to remove to Canada and set up his press there, and had shown interest in circularizing the States and inducing the Hessians to desert,[26] but unfortunately failed to respond to this timely suggestion. A resolution which was considered and laid on the table included a proviso that any material published must be sent to Congress for perusal in order to make sure that it promoted the public welfare.[27] This clause points to fear of the army as the chief reason for hesitation.

In 1781 the southern army felt a similar need. Henry Lee upon leaving North Carolina in April pointed out to Greene the need of a public press: "the proper communication of events," he commented, "would tend very much to stir up the patriotism of the people."[28] In July Greene tried to induce one Thomas Walters to establish his press at Charlotte or Salisbury. "Nothing will contribute more to the recovery of these Southern States," he argued, "than a proper channel to convey intelligence to the people; for want of which they are kept in ignorance and subject to every British imposition."[29] A week later he tried to interest Congress in the project. "A printing press is exceedingly wanted," he wrote to Congress.[30] Lafayette pleaded with Governor Thomas Nelson of Virginia for a light press at the State capital.[31] But these suggestions, like Washington's, were evidently fruitless.

We may conclude that pulpit, platform, and press were powerful propaganda agencies for the Revolution, but that they were poorly organized for army use. The generals' suggestions for an improved system, had they been adopted, would have given a still more decided impetus to morale. Much of the responsibility for maintaining morale, in fact, rested upon the shoulders of the army officers.

An examination of the attitudes and methods of the officers reveals the fact that religious enthusiasm was by no means confined to the chaplains. Possessed of the conviction that the war was a holy crusade against a cruel oppressor, many officers tried to keep the camp "free from every accursed thing" such as profanity and gambling, so that God might intervene in behalf of the patriot cause.[32] Military journals, letters, and orderly books are full of such faith and purpose.[33] Washington had profound confidence in the justice of his cause, conscientiously tried to keep the army pure, and counted strongly on providential aid.[34] There was much reliance on days of public thanksgiving, fasting, and prayer to promote repentance, to secure divine blessing, and to strengthen morale.[35]

It is further apparent that officers used every possible appeal in order to arouse patriotism. They quickly realized the need for independence as a definite goal which would commit the soldiery to a life-and-death struggle with all bridges burned behind them.[36] The Declaration of Independence was overwhelmingly convincing to the vast majority of men in arms.[37] Everywhere the army received the Declaration with loud cheers.[38] Thereafter the officers continually warned both soldiers and civilians against any relaxation of effort, with particular emphasis on the deceitfulness of British offers of peace.[39] Boundless vilification of the enemy formed the mainstay of the propaganda to which the army was treated.[40]

Tory "fifth column" activity must constantly be exposed. Every enemy post, every Loyalist inhabitant near the camp, and every prisoner of war in American hands was a real or potential source of dangerous British propaganda.[41] Washington was baffled by enemy agents and publications that wormed their way into patriot circles under various guises.[42]

As in other wars, atrocity stories played their part. By a combination of facts, half-truths, and lies, the British were represented as delighting in the defilement of churches, in the murder of the innocent, the ravishing of mothers and young girls, and the torture of prisoners. Hessians were veritable monsters.[43] British predatory expeditions during the latter half of the war produced an especially rich crop of atrocity charges.[44] The sending of the detested "arch traitor," Arnold, into Virginia in 1781 was a blunder unequaled in its folly during the entire war.[45] In fact, terrorism in any form, whether used by Lord Dunmore, Tryon, or Cornwallis, or by unmanageable Hessians and Indians and free-lance Tory officers, stiffened patriot resistance and thus defeated its own purpose.[46]

So apparent was the stimulating effect of every British outrage that American army officers actually feared any kindness from the enemy. Sailors captured by Carleton on Lake Champlain were carefully kept from mingling with the soldiers lest their tales of British generosity work mischief in the army.[47] Washington hoped that Howe's conduct in the Philadelphia campaign late in 1777 would resemble the former rigorous policy so that hatred would continue to burn against the invader.[48] Congress, however, failed to use the opportunity presented for systematic publication of atrocity literature. Plans were considered for extensive manifestoes and for a school book embodying the whole story of enemy cruelties, but the only actual results were sundry pamphlets, protests, and threats of retaliation.[49] Army officers, however, took pains to acquaint their men with all the horrid details, songs of hate were widely used in camp, and the chaplains thundered vengeance in sermon, hymn, and prayer. Such propaganda certainly had considerable effect on the army.[50]

It is apparent that civilian efforts were so inadequate that they could never have brought home to the soldiery the ultra-patriotic view of the war if army officers had not lent their full influence to that end. Hence a brief summary of the propaganda materials in orderly books is needed to make the story complete. There we find the exhortations that were brought directly to the men day after day and that must often have proved to be the decisive factor in forming army opinion. Therein appeared the official announcements of successes won in every theater of war, embellished with encouraging comments. Supplemented by occasional harangues from eloquent officers in person, and buttressed by the personal influence of the authors, general orders challenged the men to high devotion and courage. The righteousness of the cause and the glory of victory were contrasted to the villainy of the enemy and their sure defeat.[51] The advantages of army service as compared to civilian life were painted in glowing colors.[52] George Weedon, for example, aroused the Virginia militia by a diatribe on Arnold's raids.[53] Putnam appealed to history to show how the forefathers had fled British persecution and had suffered in a hostile wilderness, and thus called his men to valor against renewed oppression.[54] Officers constantly minimized the hardships the men must undergo, commended their fortitude, and pointed to a rosy future.[55] Some officers, including Steuben, Arnold, Clark, Wayne, Greene, Lafayette, and Washington, possessed personal magnetism that deeply inspired their troops.[56]

Washington's remarkable influence over the army is an excellent illustration of what the best officers could do for morale. His calmness, integrity, intense patriotism, and lofty faith held him firm through inconceivable discouragements, and enabled men to cling to him as to a rock.[57] He was master of the more subtle propaganda devices as well as of the more obvious methods. One of his ruses was the propagation in camp of rumors which he knew to be false but which were favorable to morale—a trick sometime played through seemingly casual conversation intended for the servants' ears.[58] Another device was to conceal the complete paralysis of his supply services by ordering preparations for a march.[59] He employed every conceivable device, from hints to threats, to steel his men against hardship and the shock of battle.[6 Commendation for every worthy act of officer or private wa prompt and unstinted. Needed reproof was not spared.[61] He wa unwearied in depicting the horrors of enemy atrocities and the sanctity of the American cause.[62] He won the complete confidence of the soldiers, and was the idol of the army.[63] A message from him could stir an entire corps to enthusiasm.[64] His appearance in camp would produce general jubilation.[65] His influence saved the day at Monmouth and held the army together at Valley Forge.[6 It is hard to see how the Revolution could have succeeded without him.

The evidence points to the conclusion that Revolutionary army morale rested largely on a conception of the war as a crusade divinely blessed against a cruel oppressor. Hatred of the enemy and a tenacious desire for liberty were the dominating motives of the soldier. And, in default of a well-organized civilian propaganda system, maintenance of morale rested to a large degree on the influence and ingenuity of the best army officers.

☆ V ☆

# *Conclusion*

A few general observations may be made on the basis of the resent investigation.

In the first place, problems of army morale during the Ameri-an Revolution were those inherent in an irregular, fluctuating orce. The cohesion of highly organized regular troops was large-y lacking. Morale—always one of the more difficult and unpre-ictable factors with which military leaders are concerned—was herefore doubly precarious in the Revolutionary army. With oldiers recruited more or less haphazardly, serving mostly for rief terms, inadequately trained, and poorly provisioned, the pos-ibility of discouragement and of panic was greatly increased. evolutionary morale therefore exhibited violent contrasts between ne courage and abject misbehavior, between the highest elation nd the deepest dejection. The whole basis of morale, in brief, as more uncertain than it usually is in a regular standing army.

A second outstanding fact is that Revolutionary morale was onditioned by widespread fear of militarism. The difficulty of ecuring recruits because of civilian indifference or opposition, nd the soldiers' resentment against strict discipline, conspired to roduce much insubordination. Officers and men were subjected civilian suspicion and neglect which were extremely discourag-ng. The army was left practically to shift for itself in the midst of a hostile environment, and inevitably there were desperate resorts to violence in order to secure reasonable provision from the public. Thus a multitude of officers and men left the army in despair, and effective apprehension of such deserters was impossible. Fear of militarism, in short, made the maintenance of an orderly and enthusiastic fighting force almost impossible.

Furthermore, Revolutionary army morale was personally motivated to an unusual degree. It could not be maintained by regimentation. Patriot troops were strongly individualistic and quick to resent domination, but were willing to suffer much in order to achieve the liberty they coveted. The soldier who remained long in the army was likely to exhibit an astonishing capacity for idealism and endurance. Trying circumstances tended to winnow the force to an irreducible minimum of fiercely determined men. Seldom have soldiers undergone such hardship for the sake of a principle.

And so it happened that the maintenance of army morale rested in a very large measure upon the shoulders of a few faithful officers. Organization of propaganda and of other devices for sustaining morale was lamentably defective, for the public almost totally neglected the matter. If morale were to be preserved, the officers must see to it. And they must solve the problem with few implements other than their own personal influence. The task of conducting a rebellion is always risky and difficult, and usually devolves largely upon an outstanding leader with a few loyal subordinates who are able to inspire popular confidence. The American Revolution, continued as it was for many years against overwhelming odds, presented an unusual opportunity to officers of strong character and magnetic personality. Great credit is therefore due to Washington and his faithful colleagues, without whom morale would have collapsed and the Revolution would have failed.

*REFERENCES*

# I: Physical Factors

## THE QUALITY OF TROOPS

1. Charles K. Bolton, *The Private Soldier under Washington* (1902), p. 13.

2. John C. Fitzpatrick (editor), *The Writings of George Washington from the Original Manuscript Sources 1745-1799* (37 vols., 1931-1940), vol. VI, pp. 110, 181. Hereafter cited as *Writings of Washington.*

3. Benjamin Trumbull to Washington, Aug. 13, 1776, in Peter Force (editor), *American Archives* (9 vols., 1837-1853), 5th series, vol. I, p. 936.

4. Connecticut Historical Society *Collections* (24 vols., 1860-1932), vol. XII, pp. 242-259; E. B. O'Callaghan (editor), *Documents Relating to the Colonial History of the State of New York* (15 vols., 1853-1887), vol. XV, pp. 166-173; *Pennsylvania Archives* (101 vols., 1853-1914), 5th series, vol. III, pp. 435, 644-662. Only Connecticut rolls show marital status.

5. *Writings of Washington,* vol. XVII, p. 323.

6. Claude H. Van Tyne, *The War of Independence* (1929), p. 108; John M. Palmer, *General von Steuben* (1937), p. 152.

7. Emory Upton, *The Military Policy of the United States* (1912), p. 59.

8. Upton, *op. cit.,* 59.

9. Albert S. Batcheller and others (editors), *Laws of New Hampshire* (8 vols., 1904-1920), vol. IV, p. 77; Richard P. Upton, *Revolutionary New Hampshire* (1936), p. 95.

10. *Writings of Washington,* vol. XIX, p. 409; *ibid.,* vol. XXIV, p. 176.

11. *Ibid.,* vol. V, p. 111. John Adams declared that none but "the

meanest, idlest, most intemperate and worthless"—and those only to th number of a single regiment—could be obtained in New England to serv for the duration of the war. Charles F. Adams (editor), *The Works o John Adams* (10 vols., 1850-1856), vol. III, p. 48.

12. Worthington C. Ford and others (editors), *Journals of the Conti nental Congress, 1774-1789* (34 vols., 1908-1937), vol. VIII, pp. 262, 343 Hereafter cited as *Journals of Congress.* See also Hugh Jameson, *Th Organization of the Militia of the Middle States, 1775-1781* (unpublishe thesis in University of Michigan Library), p. 73.

13. O'Callaghan, *op. cit.*, vol. XV, p. 35; Massachusetts Historica Society *Collections* (78 vols., 1806-1939), 7th series, vol. II, p. 91.

14. Noah Brooks, *Henry Knox, a Soldier of the Revolution* (1900) p. 70; Charles J. Stillé, *Major-General Anthony Wayne and the Penn sylvania Line in the Continental Army* (1893), p. 44.

15. *Writings of Washington,* vol. XXI, p. 401.

16. George W. Greene, *The Life of Nathanael Greene* (3 vols., 1871) vol. II, p. 110; Jameson, *op cit.*, passim.

17. Nathanael Greene to Thomas Jefferson, Feb. 15, 1781, in Green Papers; Greene to Joseph Reed, May 4, 1781, *ibid.* Citations to the Green Papers, unless otherwise stated, indicate those in the William L. Clement Library at Ann Arbor. See also Greene to Thomas Sumter, Jan. 8, 1781 in Sumter Papers (2 vols., Library of Congress).

18. *Writings of Washington,* vol. III, p. 316.

19. George Stubblefield's orderly book in Virginia Historical So ciety *Collections,* new series, vol. VI (1887), p. 171. Tench Tilghman complained of the troops from New York City as "mostly old disbanded Regulars and low lived foreigners." See his journal in Samuel A. Harri son (editor), *Memoir of Lieutenant Colonel Tench Tilghman* (1876), p 97.

20. *Writings of Washington,* vol. VII, p. 495; *ibid.*, vol. VIII, p. 136

21. *Ibid.*, vol. VIII, p. 264, and vol. X, p. 230.

22. *Ibid.*, vol. XI, p. 337. The corps of sappers, which Washington considered as something of an engineering school, was likewise closed to foreigners. *Ibid.*, vol. XII, p. 40.

23. Benjamin F. Stevens (editor), *Facsimiles of Manuscripts in European Archives Relating to America* (25 vols., 1889-1898), no. 2094.

24. George Bancroft, *History of the United States from the Dis-overy of the American Continent*, vol. X (1874), pp. 415-417. Bancroft oubtless exaggerated the importance of this factor.

25. *Pennsylvania Archives*, 2nd series, vol. XI, pp. 53-70; *ibid.*, 5th eries, vol. III, pp. 644, 662.

26. *Ibid.*, 5th ser., vol. III, pp. 978-983. Almost half of some Mary-and corps were foreign-born. Bernard Steiner and others (editors), *Ar-hives of Maryland* (46 vols., 1883-1929), vol. XVIII, pp. 36, 54-57.

27. Edmund C. Burnett (editor), *Letters of the Members of the Con-inental Congress* (8 vols., 1921-1936), vol. V, p. 544.

28. *Writings of Washington*, vol. VIII, pp. 56, 78.

29. Greene, *op. cit.*, vol. I, p. 559. Cf. *Journals of Congress*, vol. X, . 203, note 1.

30. *Archives of Maryland*, vol. XLVII, p. 196; William L. Saunders nd Walter Clark (editors), *North Carolina Records* (26 vols., 1886-1905), ol. XXIV, pp. 33, 158, 268.

31. *North Carolina Records*, vol. XXIV, p. 156; Robert W. Gibbes, *)ocumentary History of the American Revolution* (3 vols., 1855), vol. II, . 46; *ibid.*, vol. III, p. 249.

32. Greene to Abner Nash, Apr. 13, 1781, in Greene Papers.

33. Claude H. Van Tyne, *The Loyalists in the American Revolution* 1902), p. 273.

34. Bolton, *op. cit.*, p. 39. Charles Lee, whose statements must al-vays be taken with reserve, said that " a very great part" of Georgia's :500 militia in 1776 were disaffected. *Lee Papers* (4 vols., 1871-1874), ol. II, p. 242.

35. *Writings of Washington*, vol. VI, p. 198. These recruiting in-tructions were repeated on Jan. 13, 1777: *ibid.*, vol. VII, p. 7.

36. *Ibid.*, vol. XI, pp. 253, 254.

37. Jared Sparks (editor), *Correspondence of the American Revo-ution* (4 vols., 1853), vol. III, p. 168.

38. Letters to Greene from Sumter (Jan. 2, 1782), from Anthony Vayne (Jan. 25, 1782), and from Alexander Martin (Feb. 10, 1782), in ;reene Papers; Greene to Washington, Aug. 12, 1782, *ibid.*; Thomas ßalch (editor), *Papers Relating Chiefly to the Maryland Line during the ?evolution* (1857), p. 126.

39. Greene to Robert Morris, Aug. 13, 1782, in Morris Papers.

40. *Journals of Congress,* vol. IV, p. 105 (Jan. 31, 1776).

41. *Ibid.,* vol. X, p. 203; H. R. McIlwaine (editor), *Journals of the Council of the State of Virginia* (2 vols., 1931-1932), vol. I, p. 9.

42. *Journals of Congress,* vol. XI, p. 522; *Writings of Washington* vol. XI, p. 424; *Laws of the State of New York* (5 vols., 1886-1887), vol I, p. 84; James Mitchell and Henry Flanders (editors), *The Statutes at Large of Pennsylvania from 1682 to 1801* (14 vols., 1896-1909), vol. X pp. 164, 191, 260; *North Carolina Records,* vol. XXIV, pp. 386, 414; Thomas Cooper and D. J. McCord (editors), *Statutes at Large of South Carolina* (9 vols., 1836-1841), vol. IV, p. 514.

43. *Writings of Washington,* vol. VI, pp. 198, 310, 317; *ibid.,* vol VII, p. 7, etc.; Washington Papers (in Library of Congress) under dates of Aug. 25, 1775, and Feb. 14, 1778. His warnings were directed especially at Massachusetts and Pennsylvania.

44. *Writings of Washington,* vol. XI, p. 81; *ibid.,* vol. XII, p. 470 and vol. XIII, p. 41; Burnett, *op. cit.,* vol. III, pp. 279, 432.

45. *Writings of Washington,* vol. XI, p. 642, and vol. XII, pp. 73 866; Burnett, *op. cit.,* vol. III, p. 431.

## SUPPLIES

1. Bolton, *op. cit.,* p. 121; Force, *op. cit.,* 4th series, vol. II, p. 906.

2. Force, *op. cit.,* 4th series, vol. II, pp. 1690, 1702; *ibid.,* 5th series vol. I, pp. 138, 178, 1166; Stephen Bull to Henry Laurens, Aug. 18, 1775 in Greene Papers. See a return of arms for the Pennsylvania line, June 13 1779, in U. S. Revolution: Miscellaneous Manuscripts (6 vols., in Library of American Antiquarian Society).

3. Van Tyne, *War of Independence,* p. 421.

4. *Writings of Washington,* vol. XV, p. 4; *ibid.,* vol. XVI, p. 184 and vol. XIX, p. 116; Edward Hand to Board of War, from Ft. Pitt, Feb 12, 1778, in Hand Correspondence (4 vols. in Library of Congress).

5. *Calendar of Virginia State Papers* (11 vols., 1875-1893), vol. I p. 385; Georgia Historical Society *Collections,* vol. V (1902), part 2, p 46. Greene's correspondence is full of this subject.

6. Henry Lee to Greene, Apr. 2, 1781, in Greene, *op. cit.,* vol. III p. 216.

# REFERENCES


7. Soldiers' journals emphasize especially the lack of food. See, e.g., one in Essex Institute *Historical Collections* (75 vols., 1859-1939), vol. XLVIII, pp. 51, 52; also Samuel Armstrong's journal (in Library of New England Historical and Genealogical Society), Dec. 20 and 23, 1777.

8. Greene, *op. cit.*, vol. I, p. 97; Force, *op. cit.*, 5th series, vol. I, p. 638.

9. *Ibid.*, vol. I, p. 771, and vol. III, p. 638; *Writings of Washington*, vol. VII, pp. 189, and vol. VIII, p. 135.

10. *Ibid.*, vol. VIII, p. 441. Milk was a luxury. See anonymous orderly book in Library of Rhode Island Historical Society, covering period May 3, 1775, to Mar. 31, 1776, under date of June 4, 1775.

11. *Writings of Washington*, vol. X, pp. 82, 177, 392, 461.

12. *Ibid.*, vol. XVII, pp. 273, 312, 347, 467.

13. *Ibid.*, vol. XII, pp. 122, 277; *ibid.*, vol. XVI, pp. 188, 404; *ibid.*, vol. XVIII, pp. 251, 413, etc. Cf. letter of officers to Washington, May 30, 1783, in Washington Papers.

14. Force, *op. cit.*, 4th series, vol. III, p. 46; *ibid.*, 5th series, vol. I. pp. 451, 454, 616; *Orderly Book of the Northern Army* (Munsell's Historical Series, no. 3, published 1859), pp. 106-107.

15. John Topham's journal in *Magazine of History*, vol. XIII (1916), p. 105; Caleb Haskell's journal in *ibid.*, vol. XXII (1923), p. 81.

16. Jameson, *op. cit.*, pp. 219-222.

17. Daniel Brodhead's letters from Ft. Pitt, Oct. 17, 1780, Nov. 2 and 3, 1780, and Dec. 14, 1780, in Force Transcripts, Miscellaneous Manuscripts, in Library of Congress.

18. *Lafayette in Virginia; Unpublished Letters from the Original Manuscripts* (1928), pp. 49, 54; Sparks, *op. cit.*, vol. III, p. 408.

19. William Johnson, *Sketches of the Life and Correspondence of Nathanael Greene* (2 vols., 1822), vol. I, pp. 487 following; John C. Hamilton (editor), *Works of Alexander Hamilton* (7 vols., 1850-1851), vol. I, p. 149.

20. Greene's letters in Greene Papers: to Steuben (Dec. 8, 1780), to George Fletcher (Dec. 26, 1780), to North Carolina Board of War (Dec. 7, 1780, and Jan. 17, 1781), etc.

21. *North Carolina Records*, vol. XV, p. 529; Greene to Robert Morris (early 1782?), in Morris Papers.

22. John Martin to Wayne, Jan. 19, 1782, in Greene Papers.

23. *Writings of Washington,* vol. VI, pp. 85, 381.

24. *Ibid.,* vol. VI, p. 420, and vol. XVII, pp. 287, 300, 304.

25. This was in October, 1777. *Ibid.,* vol. XI, p. 424.

26. *Ibid.,* vol. X, pp. 37, 41, 47; *ibid.,* vol. XI, pp. 35, 417, 453.

27. *Ibid.,* vol. XII, pp. 278, 336; Stillé, *op. cit.,* p. 156.

28. *Calendar of Virginia State Papers,* vol. II, p. 631.

29. Henry Dearborn's journal in Massachusetts Historical Societ *Proceedings* (64 vols., 1879-1939), 2nd series, vol. II, p. 284; Justin H Smith, *Our Struggle for the Fourteenth Colony* (2 vols., 1907), vol. II, p 31.

30. William B. Reed, *Life and Correspondence of Joseph Reed, Mili tary Secretary of Washington* (2 vols., 1847), vol. II, p. 128.

31. *Writings of Washington,* vol. XXII, p. 453; Charles S. Hall, *Lif and Letters of General Samuel Holden Parsons* (1905), p. 208.

32. Stillé, *op. cit.,* p. 127.

33. *Ibid.,* p. 133.

34. Charles Campbell (editor), *The Bland Papers,* vol. I (1840), pp 80, 136; William W. Hening (editor), *The Statutes at Large; Being Collection of all the Laws of Virginia* (13 vols., 1809-1823), vol. X, p. 71.

35. Henry A. Muhlenberg, *The Life of Major-General Peter Muhlen berg of the Revolutionary Army* (1849), pp. 32, 376; Steuben to Greene Dec. 15, 1780, in Greene Papers.

36. Henry Lee to Greene, Aug. 23, 1780, in Greene Papers; same to Board of War, Dec. 7, 1780, *ibid.*

37. Sparks, *op. cit.,* vol. III, p. 234.

38. Greene Papers under date of Aug. 1, 1781.

39. Greene's letters: to Peter Horry (Nov. 11 and Dec. 14, 1781) to Washington (Mar. 9, 1782), and to William Smallwood (Apr. 22 1782), *ibid.*

40. Greene to Sanford Dart, various dates in April, 1783, *ibid.*; Reed, *op. cit.,* vol. II, p. 471.

## SICKNESS

1. *Writings of Washington,* vol. I, p. 101; *ibid.,* vol. VI, p. 117; *ibid.,* vol. XIX, p. 433; Harmar's manuscript journal (William L. Clem ents Library), p. 9.

2. Octavius Pickering, *The Life of Timothy Pickering* (4 vols., 1867-1873), vol. I, p. 200.

3. James Thacher, *A Military Journal during the Revolutionary War* (2nd ed., 1827), p. 177; John Kalb to Mme. de Kalb in Friederich Kalb, *The Life of John Kalb, Major-General in the Revolutionary Army* (1884), p. 183.

4. Force, *op. cit.*, 4th series, vol. II, p. 1690.

5. Sparks, *op. cit.*, vol. I, p. 46.

6. Smith, *op. cit.*, vol. I, p. 442.

7. Justin H. Smith, *Arnold's March from Cambridge to Quebec* (1903), p. 115.

8. Haskell's journal in *Magazine of History*, vol. XXII, p. 88.

9. Force, *op. cit.*, 4th series, vol. VI, pp. 451, 453.

10. *Ibid.*, 4th series, vol. VI, p. 1069; Sparks, *op. cit.*, vol. I, pp. 231, 239, 526.

11. Force, *op. cit.*, 5th series, vol. I, pp. 375, 1073, 1114; Frederic R. Kirkland (editor), *Journal of Lewis Beebe* (1935), pp. 6, 9, 23.

12. Force, *op. cit.*, 5th series, vol. III, p. 1359. Cf. *Journal of the Rev. Ammi R. Robbins* (1850), p. 10.

13. *Writings of Washington*, vol. V, pp. 364, 497; *ibid.*, vol. XIII, p. 481; Reed, *op. cit.*, vol. I, p. 215.

14. *Writings of Washington*, vol. V, p. 439, and vol. VI, p. 30.

15. Greene to John Hancock, Oct. 10, 1776, in Greene Papers; *Journals of Congress*, vol. V, p. 836, and vol. VI, p. 965.

16. *Writings of Washington*, vol. V, p. 63, and vol. VIII, pp. 64, 149. Fear of smallpox was a potent factor, especially in Virginia. New York Historical Society *Collections* (12 vols., 1824-1928), vol. XI, p. 429; William W. Henry, *Patrick Henry: Life, Correspondence, and Speeches* (3 vols., 1891), vol. III, p. 52.

17. *Journals of Congress*, vol. VIII, p. 608; *Writings of Washington*, vol. VII, pp. 72, 409. Neglect of the wounded was notorious. Henry Knox to Henry Jackson, Jan. 2, 1777, in Chamberlain Collection, Boston Public Library.

18. *Public Papers of George Clinton* (10 vols., 1899-1914), vol. II, p. 520; Edward Field (editor), *Diary of Israel Angell* (1899), p. 39.

19. Nathan G. Goodman, *Benjamin Rush, Physician and Citizen, 1746-1813* (1934), pp. 88, 93-94.

20. Reed, *op. cit.*, vol. I, p. 361.

21. Stillé, *op. cit.*, p. 138.

22. Burnett, *op. cit.*, vol. V, p. 134; *Writings of Washington*, vol. XXIII, pp. 368, 392.

23. William Heath's letters in Force, *op. cit.*, 5th series, vol. III, p. 769, and in Massachusetts Historical Society *Collections*, 7th series, vol. IV, pp. 36, 46.

24. Barnard Elliott's orderly book in *Charleston Yearbook* (1889), p. 255.

25. Dr. John Cochran to Thomas Bond in *Magazine of American History*, vol. XII, p. 249.

26. Friederick Kapp, *The Life of Frederick William von Steuben, Major General in the Revolutionary Army* (1859), p. 367.

27. *Calendar of Virginia State Papers*, vol. II, p. 486. One officer pleaded for "56 miserable, sick, naked and starving wretches" at Cumberland Old Court House. *Ibid.*, p. 681.

28. *Ibid.*, vol. II, p. 624.

29. Greene to Congress, Dec. 28, 1780, in Greene Papers.

30. Greene to Benjamin Harrison, Jan. 20, 1781, *ibid.*

31. Greene to Congress, Apr. 1, 1781, *ibid.*; James Browne to Greene, Sept. 2, 1781, *ibid.* Congress took belated action (May 15, 1781). *Journals of Congress*, vol. XX, p. 506.

32. Greene to Congress, Sept. 3, 1781, and to Board of War, Oct. 3 1782, in Greene Papers; returns of the army at Salisbury, N. C., in 1781, *ibid.*

33. Greene to Congress, Oct. 25, 1781, in Greene Papers.

34. Greene to Morris, Dec. 19, 1782, in Morris Papers.

## WAGES

1. Revolutionary finance—that taproot of many of the difficulties discussed in this chapter—has received much attention. E.g., R. V. Harlow "Aspects of Revolutionary Finance, 1775-1783," *American Historical Review*, vol. XXXV (1930), pp. 46-68; Van Tyne, *War of Independence*, pp. 59, 115. A source of great value is Hamilton, *op. cit.*, vol. I, pp. 116-132, 161-168, 223 following.

2. *Journals of Congress*, vol. III, p. 323.

3. Massachusetts Historical Society *Collections*, 7th series, vol. IV, p. 11; Greene, *op. cit.*, vol. I, p. 177; *Writings of Washington*, vol. VI, p. 109.

4. *Writings of Washington*, vol. VI, p. 401.

5. *Ibid.*, vol. XI, p. 484; Ebenezer Huntington to Joshua Huntington, May 3, 1779, in *American Historical Review*, vol. V, p. 722.

6. William Henry Smith (editor), *The St. Clair Papers* (2 vols., 1882), vol. I, p. 461.

7. Loammi Baldwin to Mrs. Baldwin, Apr. 28, 1776, in Revolutionary War Papers, Harvard University Library; *Writings of Washington*, vol. VI, pp. 108, 112; *ibid.*, vol. X, p. 116, and vol. XI, p. 286.

8. *Writings of Washington*, vol. XVII, p. 357.

9. Kapp, *Life of Kalb*, p. 183.

10. Connecticut Historical Society *Collections*, vol. XX, p. 437.

11. Walter Stewart to Mrs. A. Stewart, May 14, 1779, in Stewart Correspondence (Force Transcripts, Library of Congress); Greene to Jeremiah Wadsworth, Mar. 13, 1779, in Greene Letters (Connecticut Historical Society).

12. Burnett, *op. cit.*, vol. V, p. 275; officers' letter to Greene, July 29, 1781, in Greene Papers.

13. Albigence Waldo's journal in *Historical Magazine*, 1st series, vol. V (1861), p. 169; Sparks, *op. cit.*, vol. II, p. 73.

14. *Writings of Washington*, vol. XI, p. 237.

15. *Ibid.*, vol. XIX, p. 411.

16. *Ibid.*, vol. V, pp. 107, 354, 382; *ibid.*, vol. VII, p. 148.

17. *Calendar of Virginia State Papers*, vol. I, p. 595, and vol. II, p. 630.

18. Greene's letters to Jethro Sumner (Apr. 19, 1781), to Board of War (Aug. 18, 1781), and to Horry (Dec. 14, 1781), in Greene Papers.

19. Washington to Morris, Mar. 9, 1782, in Morris Papers; Greene to Smallwood, Apr. 22, 1782, *ibid.* For conditions in the North, see Benedict Arnold's letter in Maine Historical Society *Collections* (43 vols., 1865-1916), 1st series, vol. I, p. 498, and in Sparks, *op. cit.*, vol. I, p. 504.

20. *Writings of Washington*, vol. XXVI, pp. 186, 239-241, 286. Illuminating petitions from officers appear in *St. Clair Papers*, vol. I, p. 573, and *Journals of Congress*, vol. XXIV, p. 291.

## *REFERENCES*

# *II: Psychological Factors*

### PROVINCIALISM


1. Greene, *op. cit.*, vol. III, pp. 66, 325. It was not until Oct. 9, 1779, that New York allowed her militia to serve outside the State for three months instead of the customary forty days, and in 1782 her three-year militia could not be ordered out of the State: *Laws of New York*, vol. I, p. 159; *Writings of Washington*, vol. XXIV, p. 470.

2. Van Tyne, *War of Independence*, p. 405; R. F. Upton, *op. cit.*, p. 105.

3. Burnett, *op. cit.*, vol. II, p. 395; *Journals of Congress*, vol. VIII, p. 509 (June 30, 1777).

4. Connecticut Historical Society *Collections*, vol. II, p. 246.

5. Benedict Arnold's letter of June 24, 1775, in Autographs, U. S. Revolution, in Library of American Antiquarian Society.

6. *Public Records of the Colony of Connecticut* (15 vols., 1850-1890), vol. XV, p. 136.

7. Burnett, *op. cit.*, vol. I, p. 421.

8. *Writings of Washington*, vol. XXI, p. 32, and vol. XXV, p. 321.

9. *Ibid.*, vol. VII, p. 469 (Apr. 25, 1777).

10. *Ibid.*, vol. XI, p. 440.

11. Greene's letter of July, 1775, in Greene, *op. cit.*, vol. I, p. 103.

12. *Ibid.*, vol. I, p. 181.

13. Greene to Nicholas Cooke, July 22, 1776, in Greene Papers.

14. *Writings of Washington*, vol. V, p. 361; Sparks, *op. cit.*, vol. I, p. 242.

15. *Writings of Washington*, vol. V, p. 361.

16. *Writings of Washington*, vol. III, pp. 433, 450. In the course of time he changed his attitude. "I do not believe that any of the states produce better men," he wrote on Jan. 22, 1777: *ibid.*, vol. VI, p. 53.

17. *Ibid.*, vol. IV, p. 73.

18. *Ibid.*, vol. VI, p. 405.

19. *Ibid.*, vol. VI, pp. 270, 273; John W. Jordan (editor), *Orderly Book of the Pennsylvania State Regiment of Foot* (1898), p. 44.

20. For typical examples see Connecticut Historical Society *Collections*, vol. II, p. 287, and Burnett, *op. cit.*, vol. I, pp. xx, 142.

21. *Public Papers of George Clinton*, vol. II, pp. 158-161; Knox to Jackson, Aug. 25, 1777, in Chamberlain Collection, Boston Public Library.

22. *Writings of Washington*, vol. XII, pp. 229, 232.

23. *Ibid.*, vol. XIX, p. 413.

## DISCIPLINE

1. *Ibid.*, vol. III, p. 371. John Trumbull characterized it as "but an assemblage of brave, enthusiastic, undisciplined country lads," with most of the officers as ignorant of military life as the men were. *Autobiography, Reminiscences and Letters of John Trumbull, from 1756 to 1841* (1841), p. 18.

2. James Roberts' manuscript orderly book (Library of Congress) under date of Sept. 10, 1776; *Writings of Washington*, vol. III, pp. 331, 374; *ibid.*, vol. XVIII, p. 71.

3. Greene, *op. cit.*, vol. I, p. 137.

4. Smith, *Our Struggle for the Fourteenth Colony*, vol. I, p. 335.

5. Smith, *Arnold's March*, pp. 115, 142.

6. The first Articles of War are in *Journals of Congress*, vol. II, pp. 111-122 (June 30, 1775). The revised code is in *ibid.*, vol. V, pp. 788-807 (Sept. 20, 1776). A few amendments were made on Nov. 7, 1775. *Ibid.*, vol. III, pp. 331-334.

7. *Ibid.*, vol. XI, p. 465.

8. *Writings of Washington*, vol. XI, pp. 132, 211, 328, 363, and vol. XXIV, p. 322; Palmer, *op. cit.*, pp. 140 following. Jean Ternant attempted a similar service for the southern army. Greene to Steuben, Dec. 9, 1782, in Greene Papers.

9. *Writings of Washington*, vol. XII, pp. 167, 171, and vol. XVII, p. 198.

10. Above, pp. 89-90; *Writings of Washington,* vol. XII, p. 349. Many illuminating comments on pardons appear in *ibid.:* e.g., vol. IX, p. 30, and vol. XXII, p. 455.

11. For interesting examples see David Avery's manuscript journal (Connecticut Historical Society) under date of Nov. 4, 1778, and Ebenezer Parkman's manuscript journal (American Antiquarian Society) under date of Feb. 19, 1780.

12. Several examples appear in *Writings of Washington:* e.g., vol. VI, pp. 90, 102, and vol. XII, pp. 313, 344, 348.

13. Baron von Steuben, *Regulations for the Order and Discipline of the Troops of the United States,* part I (1800), p. 145; Almon W. Lauber (editor), *Orderly Books of the Fourth New York and Second New York Regiments* (1932), p. 563.

14. Greene, *op. cit.,* vol. I, p. 98.

15. Sparks, *op. cit.,* vol. I, p. 469.

16. Palmer, *op. cit.,* p. 157.

17. On Sept. 28, 1779: Kapp, *Life of Steuben,* p. 236.

18. *Writings of Washington,* vol. X, p. 396, and vol. XVIII, p. 17.

19. Connecticut Historical Society *Collections,* vol. I, pp. 171, 175; Arnold's memorandum book in *Pennsylvania Magazine of History,* vol. VIII (1884), p. 373.

20. Stillé, *op. cit.,* p. 55; Southern Historical Association *Publications* (11 vols., 1897-1907), vol. XI, p. 200. Numerous examples appear in *Writings of Washington* and the Greene Papers.

21. Steuben's letter of Dec. 18, 1780, in Kapp, *Life of Steuben,* p. 356; Martin to Greene, Nov. 17, 1782, in Greene Papers. Large numbers of officers were disciplined for offenses of all kinds. Of some 1500 offenses (other than desertion) penalized by courts martial—cases selected at random from a wide range of orderly books and journals—we find fully 30% committed by commissioned and non-commissioned officers. See, e.g., *Pennsylvania Archives,* 5th series, vol. III, pp. 469-474, 607-610. For cases of cowardice: Christopher Greene's manuscript orderly book (Rhode Island Historical Society), entries for Oct. 31 and Nov. 8, 1776; Horatio Gates' manuscript orderly book (Library of Congress), Aug. 1 and Oct. 16, 1776. Some officers were cashiered more than once: *Writings of Washington,* vol. XVIII, p. 480.

22. Charles Coffin, *The Lives and Services of Major General John Thomas, Colonel Thomas Knowlton, Colonel Alexander Scammell, Major General Henry Dearborn* (1845), p. 92.

23. *Writings of Washington*, vol. XVIII, p. 71.

24. *Ibid.*, vol. XIX, p. 410.

25. *Journals of Congress*, vol. III, p. 352, and vol. V, p. 805; *Writings of Washington*, vol. IV, p. 124.

26. Ebenezer Huntington's manuscript orderly book (Library of Congress), Feb. 14, 1780; Charles F. Adams (editor), *Familiar Letters of John Adams and His Wife Abigail Adams, during the Revolution* (1876), p. 209.

27. Governor Thomas Burke to Greene, Aug. 9, 1781, in Greene Papers; Governor Nathan Brownson to Greene, Oct. 13, 1781, in Greene Papers, Library of Congress.

28. Greene, *op. cit.*, vol. III, p. 545; Reed, *op. cit.*, vol. II, p. 349.

29. *Writings of Washington*, vol. V, p. 499, and vol. VI, pp. 39, 110-111.

30. *Ibid.*, vol. XI, p. 236, and vol. XVI, p. 67.

31. *Journals of Congress*, vol. V, pp. 781, 784; Judge Advocate John Laurance to Washington, Feb. 5, 1778, in Washington Papers.

32. Hamilton to James Duane, Sept. 3, 1780, in Hamilton, *op. cit.*, vol. I, p. 150.

33. Above, p. 33.

34. George M. Wrong, *Canada and the American Revolution* (1935), p. 324; *Writings of Washington*, vol. IX, pp. 17, 139; *ibid.*, vol. XXV, pp. 132, 139.

35. *Writings of Washington*, vol. IX, pp. 2, 28, 46, 126; *ibid.*, vol. XV, p. 50.

36. Walter H. Mohr, *Federal Indian Relations, 1774-1788* (1933), pp. 69-71; Francis Marion's orderly book in Gibbes, *op. cit.*, vol. II, p. 64.

37. Many cases occur in *Writings of Washington*. Cf. the manuscript orderly book of the 2nd Massachusetts Regiment, kept by William Torrey and Luther Bailey (24 vols., Library of Congress). By 1783 Washington was convinced that rum should even be eliminated from the regular rations. *Writings of Washington*, vol. XXVI, p. 385.

38. Above, pp. 39-42.

39. It cannot be assumed that more severe discipline would have prevented all such trouble. Mutiny was not unknown in the British army during the American War, although discipline there was much more rigorous than under Washington. John W. Fortescue, *A History of the British Army* (14 vols., 1911-1935), vol. III, p. 291.

40. Emory Upton, *op. cit.*, p. 16.

41. Burnett, *op. cit.*, vol. I, pp. 208, 360; *ibid.*, vol. II, p. viii; *Writings of Washington*, vol. VI, p. 401, and passim.

42. See, e.g., Burnett, *op. cit.*, vol. V, pp. 223, 239, and Charlemagne Tower, *The Marquis de La Fayette in the American Revolution* (2 vols., 1895), vol. II, p. 261.

43. Reed, *op. cit.*, vol. I, p. 266, and vol. II, p. 372; David Humphreys to Greene, May 30, 1780, Greene Papers.

44. Manuscript journal of Samuel Weld (Rhode Island Historical Society), entry for Apr. 6, 1776, and that of Algernon Roberts (Sparks Manuscripts, vol. XLVIII, Harvard University), for Aug., 1776. Examples of pertinent legislation are in *Journals of Congress*, vol. V, p. 591, and Hening, *op. cit.*, vol. X, p. 335. For typical army orders, see those of William Heath for Nov. 11, 1776, in Heath Papers (27 vols., in Library of Massachusetts Historical Society).

45. *Writings of Washington*, vol. XIII, p. 105, and vol. XVII, p. 222.

46. Kapp, *Life of Kalb*, p. 143.

47. *Writings of Washington*, vol. XIII, p. 383.

48. State laws on the subject could not be enforced. Five armies such as he possessed, declared Washington, could not have stopped the trade with New York City. *Ibid.*, vol. XXVI, p. 242.

49. *Public Papers of George Clinton*, vol. IV, pp. 383, 504; Gilbert Chinard (editor), *Letters of Lafayette and Jefferson* (1929), pp. 27, 37.

50. Massachusetts Historical Society *Collections*, 7th series, vol. V, p. 242.

51. *Public Papers of George Clinton*, vol. IV, p. 688.

52. *Ibid.*, vol. I, pp. 525 following. Arnold's refusal to serve under Benjamin Hinman in 1775 prompted a mutiny among some of his men. Force, *op. cit.*, 4th series, vol. II, p. 1541.

53. Stillé, *op. cit.*, p. 55.

54. Sparks, *op. cit.*, vol. II, p. 31; Hamilton, *op. cit.*, vol. I, p. 45.

55. According to Washington, negligence on the part of officers was a contributing factor. *Writings of Washington*, vol. XIV, pp. 111-112, 259. John Sullivan administered some floggings and reduced several sergeants. John Glover's orderly book in Essex Institute *Historical Collections, vol.* V, pp. 125-127; David Bradish's manuscript orderly book (in William L. Clements Library), entries for Sept. 23, 1778, Feb. 5, 1779, and passim.

56. Massachusetts Historical Society *Collections*, 7th series, vol. IV, p. 299; *Writings of Washington*, vol. XIV, p. 483.

57. *Writings of Washington*, vol. XVI, p. 139.

58. *Ibid.*, vol. XVII, p. 163.

59. *Ibid.*, p. 398.

60. B. Ball to Walter Stewart, Feb. 15, 1780, in Stewart Correspondence.

61. *Writings of Washington*, vol. XIX, pp. 36, 45. L. C. Hatch was evidently incorrect in stating that the Ticonderoga rising of 1777 was the only one before 1781 which resulted in bloodshed. L. C. Hatch, *The Administration of the American Revolutionary Army* (1904), p. 124.

62. James Clinton to Washington, July 10, 1781, in Washington Papers; John C. Fitzpatrick (editor), *The Diaries of George Washington* (4 vols., 1925), vol. II, p. 235. Washington on Aug. 10 confirmed a death sentence on one Edmund Burke for his part in the July mutiny. *Writings of Washington*, vol. XXII, p. 487.

63. Caleb Stark (editor), *Memoir and Official Correspondence of General John Stark* (1860), p. 297.

64. Sparks, *op. cit.*, vol. III, pp. 454, 472, 501.

65. Paul L. Ford (editor), *The Writings of Thomas Jefferson* (10 vols., 1892-1899), vol. II, p. 465, and vol. III, p. 24; *Illinois Historical Collections* (26 vols., 1903-1934), vol. XIX, p. xxxvi.

66. Worthington C. Ford (editor), *Warren-Adams Letters* (2 vols., 1917-1925), vol. I, p. 107; Hatch, *op. cit.*, p. 96.

67. Lacking food and clothing, the men planned to go to Hartford to threaten the legislature. Israel Putnam dissuaded them. Hall, *op. cit.*, p. 208; *Writings of Washington*, vol. XIV, pp. 20-21.

68. Reed, *op. cit.*, vol. II, p. 201; *Writings of Washington*, vol. XVIII, pp. 424 following.

69. Hall, *op. cit.*, pp. 321, 324, 382-386; Ebenezer Huntington's letter in *American Historical Review*, vol. V, p. 727.

70. Massachusetts Historical Society *Collections*, 7th series, vol. V, p. 373; *Writings of Washington*, vol. XXIV, pp. 227, 248.

71. Greene's letters to John Mathews and John Kean, Mar. 30, 1782, and to Wayne, Congress, etc., on various dates in April, 1782, in Greene Papers; Wayne to Greene, Apr. 28, 1782, *ibid.* The plot was to march their officers to Dorchester and to give them up to the enemy if grievances were not redressed. Greene to Congress, May 18, 1782, and to Benjamin Harrison, May 19, 1782, *ibid.*

72. Reports of discontent in the North also had their effect. Moreover, the men claimed discharges and feared that their horses would be taken at the end of the war. Greene Papers under dates of Mar. 16 and 31, 1783, and Apr. 2, 3, and 7, 1783.

73. Greene to Benjamin Lincoln, May 17, 1783, *ibid.*; Joseph Eggleston to Greene, May 12 and 22, 1783, in Greene Papers, Library of Congress.

74. Greene to Lincoln, May 17 and June 3, 1783, in Greene Papers, William L. Clements Library.

75. Stillé, *op. cit.*, pp. 238-262; *Writings of Washington*, vol. XXI, pp. 57-112, 193.

76. Isaac Sherman to Loammi Baldwin, Feb. 7, 1781, in Revolutionary War Papers of Loammi Baldwin; *Writings of Washington*, vol. XXI, pp. 113, 175-176, 294.

77. Arrangements for adequate pay and clothing were a significant part of the agreement which ended the mutiny. Bolton, *op. cit.*, pp. 138-140. Washington constantly emphasized the intolerable sufferings of the men as the crux of the situation. *Writings of Washington*, vol. XXI, pp. 61, 66, 120.

78. Hamilton, *op. cit.*, vol. I, p. 209; Burnett, *op. cit.*, vol. I, pp. xix, 151, and passim.

79. The demands were similar to those of the Pennsylvania mutineers. Discontent had been serious during 1779, when the New Jersey officers set a bad example by demanding pay before they would march against the Indians—a demand later withdrawn through Washington's influence. *Writings of Washington*, vol. XV, pp. 13, 32, 43; *ibid.*, vol. XXI,

pp. 124-160, 193. A good summary appears in Hatch, *op. cit.*, pp. 138-140.

80. *Writings of Washington,* vol. XXI, pp. 154, 157, 208.

81. *Ibid.*, vol. XXII, p. 191; Ebenezer Denny's journal in Pennsylvania Historical Society *Memoirs,* vol. VII (1860), p. 237.

82. *Writings of Washington,* vol. XXV, pp. 108, 228, 448; *ibid.*, vol. XXVI, p. 213. The famous Newburgh Addresses in March, 1783, gave Congress a temporary scare and demonstrated once again the competence of Washington. Hatch, *op. cit.*, pp. 199 following.

83. The mutineers were largely men recently enlisted. A few floggings were administered, but no capital punishment was used. Two of the ringleaders escaped to Europe. Hatch, *op. cit.*, pp. 181-188. Perhaps the best contemporary account is that by Alexander Hamilton in a letter to Reed, beginning June 19, 1783, in Hamilton, *op. cit.*, vol. I, p. 384.

## BEHAVIOR IN ACTION

1. Thomas G. Frothingham, *Washington, Commander-in-Chief* (1930), pp. 58, 83; Palmer, *op. cit.*, p. 151.

2. Such superiority was the more remarkable in that scarcity of ammunition made target practice the exception rather than the rule. *Writings of Washington,* vol. VII, p. 198, and vol. VIII, pp. 108, 186; manuscript orderly book in John Hay Library (Feb. 7-Aug. 13, 1777) under date of July 24, 1777.

3. Palmer, *op. cit.*, p. 152; *Writings of Washington,* vol. XXIII, p. 147. Americans used the bayonet effectively in some battles: e.g., at the Cowpens. Daniel Morgan to Greene, Jan. 19, 1781, in Greene Papers, Library of Congress.

4. *Writings of Washington,* vol. V, p. 444.

5. *Ibid.*, vol. IV, p. 299. Henry Knox thought that the reverse at Brandywine was due to using raw recruits. Knox to Jackson, Sept. 13, 1777, in Chamberlain Collection, Boston Public Library.

6. *Writings of Washington,* vol. V, p. 390, and vol. VI, p. 28.

7. *Ibid.*, vol. VI, p. 83.

8. *Ibid.*, vol. IX, pp. 312, 336, 377; Charles Stedman, *The History of the Origin, Progress, and Termination of the American War* (2 vols., 1794), vol. II, p. 2.

9. Kapp, *Life of Steuben,* p. 236.

10. Aaron Barlow's orderly book in *American Historical Register,* vol. III (1896), p. 666; Simeon Thayer's journal in Rhode Island Historical Society *Collections,* vol. VI (1867), p. 27.

11. *Writings of Washington,* vol. VI, pp. 8, 244.

12. *Ibid.,* vol. XIX, p. 438.

13. Greene to Steuben, Apr. 27, 1781, in Greene Papers.

14. Sparks, *op. cit.,* vol. I, p. 116.

15. Smith, *Our Struggle for the Fourteenth Colony,* vol. II, pp. 319-322.

16. Force, *op. cit.,* 5th series, vol. II, p. 1012.

17. *Writings of Washington,* vol. VI, p. 58.

18. *Ibid.,* p. 146; Heath's orders, Sept. 20, 1776, in Heath Papers.

19. *Writings of Washington,* vol. IX, pp. 310, 320, 397.

20. See contemporary account in Johnson, *op. cit.,* vol. I, p. 498.

21. *Writings of Washington,* vol. V, p. 130; *ibid.,* vol. VI, p. 219; *ibid.,* vol. VII, p. 53.

23. Many instances are mentioned in *Writings of Washington:* e.g., vol. VI, p. 234, and vol. VII, pp. 122, 337. Others appear in orderly books already cited. See also R. O. Bascom (editor), *Orderly Book of Captain Ichabod Norton* (1898), p. 38, and manuscript orderly books by Charles Lee and Richard Montgomery in Library of Congress.

24. William G. Simms (editor), *The Army Correspondence of Colonel John Laurens in the years 1777-1778* (1867), p. 102.

25. Sparks, *op. cit.,* vol. III, pp. 66, 108.

26. Greene to Jefferson, Mar. 16, 1781, in Greene Papers.

27. Harrison, *op. cit.,* p. 137; *Writings of Washington,* vol. VI, p. 110.

28. Greene, *op. cit.,* vol. I, p. 276.

29. *Ibid.,* p. 275.

30. *Ibid.,* pp. 362-363.

31. Hall, *op. cit.,* p. 253; *Writings of Washington,* vol. XV, p. 423.

32. Harmar's journal, p. 59.

33. Greene's letter of Jan. 10, 1777, in Greene Papers.

34. Tower, *op. cit.,* vol. I, p. 250; *ibid.,* vol. II, p. 421; *Writings of Washington,* vol. XII, pp. 19, 130.

35. See, e.g., Thomas Sumter to Greene, July 17, 18, and 22, 1781, in Greene Papers; Francis Marion to Greene, July 29, 1781, *ibid.*

36. John C. Fitzpatrick, *George Washington Himself* (1933), p. 290; Van Tyne, *War of Independence*, p. 108.

37. Palmer, *op. cit.*, p. 248; *Writings of Washington*, vol. XIX, p. 65.

38. Greene to Steuben, Feb. 18, 1781, in Greene Papers.

39. Weedon to Greene, Oct. 17, 1780, *ibid.;* Greene to Isaac Huger (Jan. 30, 1781) and to Arthur Campbell (Feb. 26, 1781), *ibid.;* Nathanael Greene's manuscript orderly book (Rhode Island Historical Society), under date of May 15, 1781.

40. Van Tyne, *War of Independence*, p. 394.

41. Force, *op. cit.*, 4th series, vol. II, p. 1021.

42. Emory Upton, *op. cit.*, p. 2.

43. Force, *op. cit.*, 4th series, vol. II, p. 1097.

44. Sparks, *op. cit.*, vol. I, pp. 117, 500, 505.

45. Smith, *Our Struggle for the Fourteenth Colony*, vol. II, p. 147.

46. Sparks, *op. cit.*, vol. I, p. 522; Force, *op. cit.*, 5th series, vol. I, pp. 150, 214, 1194, 1195, 1245. Washington considered the battle of Long Island to have been fought "with great Resolution and bravery on the part of our Troops." *Writings of Washington*, vol. VI, p. 21.

47. *Writings of Washington*, vol. VI, pp. 63, 244, 444, 446; *ibid.*, vol. XII, p. 347; Force, *op. cit.*, 5th series, vol. II, p. 1271; *ibid.*, vol. III, pp. 472, 809.

48. Stedman, *op. cit.*, vol. I, p. 323. As to Ft. Mifflin, see Pickering, *op. cit.*, vol. I, p. 182.

49. *Writings of Washington*, vol. XII, p. 145; *ibid.*, vol. XV, p. 427, note 41; Morgan's letter to Greene, Jan. 19, 1781, in Greene Papers, Library of Congress; Herbert E. Bolton and Thomas M. Marshall, *The Colonization of North America* (1925), p. 527. Greene was particularly proud of his men's behavior at Eutaw Springs. See his letters of Sept. 11, Sept. 16, and Sept. 17, 1781, in Greene Papers. For examples of the many minor exploits revealing American valor, see Thomas C. Amory, *The Military Services and Public Life of Major-General John Sullivan of the American Revolutionary Army* (1868), pp. 119, 224; also Michael Walters' journal in J. P. MacLean (editor), Western Reserve Historical Society *Tracts*, no. 89 (1899), pp. 182-183.

## FLUCTUATIONS IN MORALE

1. A typical allusion is that by Colonel Ebenezer Huntington on Jan. 8, 1780: "Let the Virtue, the Love for the Country which filled the breast of us all in 75 be roused, if a Spark still remains. . . ." Connecticut Historical Society *Collections,* vol. XX, p. 437.

2. Carl Becker, J. M. Clark, and William E. Dodd, *The Spirit of 1776 and Other Essays* (1927), chapters I and III. Of these two chapters dealing with the Revolution, scarcely eleven pages concern events in 1776.

3. Bolton and Marshall, *op. cit.,* p. 461; Emory Upton, *op. cit.,* pp. 4-5.

4. *Writings of Washington,* vol. X, p. 363.

5. Force, *op. cit.,* 4th series, vol. II, p. 1049.

6. *Ibid.,* pp. 362, 373, 423; Nathaniel Bouton (editor), *New Hampshire Provincial Papers* (7 vols., 1867-1873), vol. VII, p. 461.

7. Connecticut Historical Society *Collections,* vol. II, pp. 220, 229. In June came the report of an Old Man's Company at Redding, Pa., with the entire force consisting of Germans from forty to ninety-seven years of age. Force, *op. cit.,* 4th series, vol. II, p. 878.

8. Essex Institute *Historical Collections,* vol. III, p. 54.

9. *Writings of Washington,* vol. III, pp. 322, 483, 512.

10. *Ibid.,* vol. IV, p. 82.

11. *Ibid.,* p. 82.

12. Emory Upton, *op. cit.,* p. 5.

13. Sydney G. Fisher, *The Struggle for American Independence* (2 vol., 1908), vol. I, p. 244.

14. Hamilton J. Eckenrode, *The Revolution in Virginia* (1916), p. 184.

15. Above, p. 13.

16. Jameson, *op. cit.,* p. 244 and appendices.

17. *American State Papers: Military Affairs,* vol. I (1832), pp. 14-19. The number for 1775 was 27,443; for 1781, 20,590. The small figure for 1775 must be considered in the light of the slowness with which plans for a Continental army got under way.

18. Cf. above, pp. 30-31.

19. *Writings of Washington,* vol. IV, p. 146; Jeremiah Fogg, *Orderly Book* (1903), p. 57.

20. Greene, *op. cit.*, vol. I, p. 139.

21. *Writings of Washington*, vol. IV, pp. 241, 300.

22. *Ibid.*, pp. 241, 300.

23. Smith, *Our Struggle for the Fourteenth Colony*, vol. II, pp. 202, 221.

24. *Ibid.*, pp. 310-312. In bad weather, declared Knox, an archangel from heaven could not have prevailed on such men to continue a single day after their time was up. Knox to Jackson, Jan. 2, 1777, in Chamberlain Collection, Boston Public Library.

25. *Writings of Washington*, vol. XIII, p. 438; *ibid.*, vol. XXII, p. 102.

26. Massachusetts Historical Society *Collections*, 7th series, vol. IV, pp. 30, 34.

27. *Writings of Washington*, vol. XIII, p. 145; *ibid.*, vol. V, p. 343.

28. *Ibid.*, vol. XXIII, p. 32, and vol. XXIV, p. 502. James Thacher observed that "amidst all the toils and hardships, there are charms in a military life." Thacher, *op. cit.*, p. 184.

29. Force, *op. cit.*, 5th series, vol. III, pp. 796-798. Washington cautiously recommended such furloughs, which might cover most of the winter. *Writings of Washington*, vol. XVII, pp. 194, 228, 281.

30. *Writings of Washington*, vol. VI, p. 347; *ibid.*, vol. XVII, p. 118, and vol. XIX, p. 405; Kapp, *Life of Steuben*, p. 243.

31. James Chambers' orderly book in *Pennsylvania Archives*, 2nd series, vol. XI, p. 460; Henry Lenn to Greene, Jan. 28, 1782, in Greene Papers.

32. *Writings of Washington*, vol. XVIII, p. 432.

33. Greene, *op. cit.*, vol. I, p. 298; *ibid.*, vol. III, p. 341.

34. New York Historical Society *Collections*, vol. XI, p. 456.

35. Hamilton, *op. cit.*, vol. I, p. 155.

36. *Writings of Washington*, vol. XIX, p. 195.

37. *Ibid.*, p. 408.

38. *Ibid.*, vol. XX, p. 146 (Oct. 10, 1780).

39. Above, pp. 45-47.

40. John Medbury's manuscript journal (Rhode Island Historical Society) under date of July 20, 1776; *Writings of Washington*, vol. IV, p. 455; *ibid.*, vol. V, pp. 238, 245, 247.

41. Allen Bowman, "The Morale of the American Army in the Latter Half of 1776," *Virginia Magazine of History and Biography*, vol. XXXIX (1931), pp. 193-205.

42. *Writings of Washington*, vol. VII, pp. 328, 334.

43. *Ibid.*, vol. XI, pp. 324, 333, 502.

44. *Ibid.*, p. 348.

45. Tower, *op. cit.*, vol. I, p. 318.

46. *Writings of Washington*, vol. XIV, p. 27.

47. *Ibid.*, vol. XI, pp. 398, 402 following; *ibid.*, vol. XIII, p. 46.

48. *Ibid.*, vol. XIII, pp. 80, 156.

49. Greene, *op. cit.*, vol. II, pp. 79, 144. Henry Knox had the same illusion. See his letters to William Knox, Sept. 8, 1778, and Oct. 5, 24, 28, in Knox Papers.

50. Harmar's journal, p. 66.

51. *Ibid.*, p. 20 (Feb. 13, 1779).

52. *Writings of Washington*, vol. XIV, p. 5; *ibid.*, vol. XV, p. 61, and vol. XVI, p. 222.

53. *Ibid.*, vol. XVI, p. 372 (Sept. 30, 1779).

54. *Ibid.*, vol. XVIII, p. 437 (May 28, 1780).

55. Lafayette's return in May, 1780, was especially cheering. *Writings of Washington*, vol. XVIII, pp. 348, 351, 356.

56. William Feltman's journal in William H. Egle (editor), *Journals and Diaries of the War of the Revolution* (*Pennsylvania Archives*, 2nd series, vol. XI, published in 1880), p. 687.

57. *Writings of Washington*, vol. XXIII, p. 341 (Nov. 15, 1781).

58. Hamilton, *op. cit.*, vol. I, p. 317.

59. Hatch, *op. cit.*, p. 4.

60. Burnett, *op. cit.*, vol. I, p. 309; *ibid.*, vol. II, p. 22; *Writings of Washington*, vol. V, pp. 52, 54, 58, 64.

61. Frothingham, *op. cit.*, p. 102.

62. Said Colonel William Malcolm: "The very thought [of abandoning New York] gives me the horrours." Force, *op. cit.*, 5th series, vol. II, p. 197.

63. *Writings of Washington*, vol. VI, pp. 4, 29.

64. Massachusetts Historical Society *Collections*, 7th series, vol. IV, p. 23; Greene, *op. cit.*, vol. I, p. 212.

65. *Public Papers of George Clinton,* vol. I, p. 353; Reed, *op. cit.,* vol. I, p. 238.

66. *Writings of Washington,* vol. VI, pp. 244, 298.

67. Bolton and Marshall, *op. cit.,* p. 489; Huntington's letter of Nov. 25, 1776, in *American Historical Review,* vol. V, p. 715.

68. *Writings of Washington,* vol. VI, p. 397. So extravagant was the popular regard for Charles Lee that his capture created a further impression of disaster. George H. Moore, *The Treason of Charles Lee* (1860), p. 67.

69. On Dec. 22, 1776, Joseph Reed had suggested "a diversion, or something more, at or about Trenton," for "something must be attempted to revive our expiring credit." Reed, *op. cit.,* vol. I, p. 272. See Washington's statement about the march to Princeton in *Writings of Washington,* vol. VI, p. 467.

70. Fitzpatrick's figure is apt: "In America the news of Trenton was like the sun breaking through heavy clouds." Fitzpatrick, *op. cit.,* p. 281.

71. Fortescue, *op. cit.,* vol. III, p. 203.

72. The Hessians had been regarded in America with something of superstitious awe. William S. Stryker, *The Battles of Trenton and Princeton* (1898), p. 221.

73. Sparks, *op. cit.,* vol. I, pp. 315, 317, 327; *Writings of Washington,* vol. VI, pp. 448, 455, 463, 504.

74. Frothingham, *op. cit.,* p. 198.

75. Greene, *op. cit.,* vol. I, pp. 398, 431; *Writings of Washington,* vol. VIII, pp. 384, 407.

76. Massachusetts Historical Society *Collections,* 7th series, vol. II, pp. 103, 112.

77. *Writings of Washington,* vol. VIII, p. 407; *ibid.,* vol. IX, pp. 16, 76.

78. Enos Hitchcock's journal in Rhode Island Historical Society *Publications,* new series, vol. VII (1899-1900), pp. 132-134, 151.

79. Frothingham, *op. cit.,* p. 188.

80. Greene, *op. cit.,* vol. I, p. 435.

81. *Writings of Washington,* vol. VI, pp. 340, 348, 352, 428.

82. Massachusetts Historical Society *Collections,* 7th series, vol. II, p. 169.

83. Burnett, *op. cit.*, vol. II, p. 545. Washington probably sent more congratulatory letters on this occasion than after any other battle, unless it be Yorktown. *Writings of Washington*, vol. IX, pp. 382, 393, 399, and passim.

84. *Ibid.*, vol. X, p. 114.

85. Greene, *op. cit.*, vol. I, p. 511. This was only a month after Saratoga.

86. Palmer, *op. cit.*, p. 16; *Writings of Washington*, vol. XII, pp. 139-148, 156-160; William S. Stryker, *The Battle of Monmouth* (1927), p. 273.

87. Colonel Lewis Morris actually wished that the enemy would attempt something and thus save the patriot army from such demoralization as Hannibal's once suffered in Capua. Morris to Greene, Feb. 16, 1779, in Greene Papers. The storming of Stony Point in July, 1779, is an example of the surprise actions undertaken to break the spell. *Writings of Washington*, vol. XV, pp. 427-432.

88. Claude H. Van Tyne, *The American Revolution*, 1776-1783 (1905), p. 302. An ineffectual effort in the next campaign, Washington predicted, would end all resistance to England. *Writings of Washington*, vol. XXI, p. 107 (Jan. 15, 1781).

89. *Writings of Washington*, vol. XVIII, p. 209. "In short we are going to the Devil as fast as possible," was Edward Hand's remark. Hand to Jasper Yeates, Sept. 10, 1780, in Hand Correspondence.

90. Frothingham terms it "the most serious defeat of the Americans in the Revolution." Frothingham, *op. cit.*, p. 310.

91. Hamilton, *op. cit.*, vol. I, p. 182; William Davidson to Jethro Sumner, Sept. 10, 1780, in Sumner Papers (2 vols., in William L. Clements Library).

92. Reed, *op. cit.*, vol. II, p. 344; Sumner's letter of Oct. 12, 1780, in Sumner Papers.

93. Greene to Congress (Dec. 28, 1780) and to Lafayette (Dec. 29, 1780) in Greene Papers; Sparks, *op. cit.*, vol. III, pp. 166, 188, 322.

94. Greene declared early in 1781 that if he should risk a general action he would stand ten chances to one of being beaten. Letter to Sumter, Feb. 9, 1781, in Greene Papers.

95. Greene's letters to Steuben (Jan. 23, 1781), to Nash (Jan. 27,

1781) and to Jefferson (Feb. 28, 1781) in *ibid.;* Marion to Greene, Jan. 27, 1781, *ibid.*

96. Greene's letters, various dates in March and May, 1781, in Greene Papers; Greene to Wadsworth, July 18, 1781, in Greene Letters, Connecticut Historical Society.

97. *Writings of Washington*, vol. XXII, p. 215; *ibid.*, vol. XXIII, p. 188. Cornwallis' surrender at Yorktown, of course, produced great rejoicing; but thereafter army morale degenerated rapidly as the men grew impatient to return home. *Letters of James McHenry to Governor Thomas Sim Lee, 1781* (1931), p. 68; Smallwood to Greene, Oct. 15, 1782, in Greene Papers, Library of Congress.

## DEVOTION TO THE CAUSE

1. Smith, *Our Struggle for the Fourteenth Colony*, vol. I, pp. 544 following.

2. Massachusetts Historical Society *Proceedings*, 2nd series, vol. II, pp. 268-270.

3. Eleazer Oswald's journal in Force, *op. cit.*, 4th series, vol. III, p. 1062.

4. Isaac Senter's journal in Pennsylvania Historical Society *Proceedings*, vol. I, no. 5 (1846), p. 18.

5. Maine Historical Society *Collections*, 1st series, vol. I, pp. 471, 477, 480, 487-490, 490-496.

6. Sparks, *op. cit.*, vol. I, p. 373; Greene, *op. cit.*, vol. I, p. 486.

7. Waldo's journal in *Historical Magazine*, 1st series, vol. V, p. 131.

8. William E. H. Lecky, *A History of England in the Eighteenth Century*, vol. IV (1888), p. 63.

9. Simms, *op. cit.*, p. 112.

10. Quoted in Tower, *op. cit.*, vol. I, p. 255.

11. Kapp, *Life of Kalb*, p. 142.

12. Palmer, *op. cit.*, p. 137.

13. *Writings of Washington*, vol. X, p. 469.

14. *Ibid.*, vol. XI, p. 291. Further evidence appears in the attachment to the service expressed in army correspondence. See, e.g., Walter Stewart to Mrs. A. Stewart, May 14, 1779, in Stewart Papers.

15. *Illinois Historical Collections*, vol. VIII, p. 140.

16. *Writings of Washington*, vol. XVII, p. 357.
17. *Ibid.*, p. 368.
18. Burnett, *op. cit.*, vol. V, p. 166.
19. New York Historical Society *Collections*, vol. XI, p. 33.
20. Brooks, *op. cit.*, p. 139.
21. At West Point, Jan. 6, 1781: Massachusetts Historical Society *Collections*, 7th series, vol. V, p. 152.
22. *Writings of Washington*, vol. XXI, pp. 157, 161.
23. Tower, *op. cit.*, vol. II, p. 379.
24. Bolton, *op. cit.*, p. 103.
25. Sparks, *op. cit.*, vol. III, p. 236.
26. Reed, *op. cit.*, vol. II, p. 350.
27. Greene to Board of War, July 28, 1781, in Greene Papers; same to Horry, Dec. 14, 1781, *ibid.*
28. Greene to Board of War, Aug. 18, 1781, *ibid.*
29. Greene to William R. Davie, Oct. 18, 1781, and to Alexander Martin, Oct. 24, 1781, *ibid.*
30. Greene to Davie, Mar. 5, 1782, *ibid.*
31. *Writings of Washington*, vol. XXV, p. 228.
32. *Ibid.*, p. 269.
33. *Ibid.*, vol. XXVI, p. 104.
34. Quoted in Fitzpatrick, *op. cit.*, p. 435. The other side of the story, of course, is to be found in the appalling desertion which at times threatened the very existence of the army, and in the mutinies which convulsed it toward the end of the war. Above, pp. 34-38 and chapter III.

# *REFERENCES*

# *III: Absenteeism and Desertion*


1. Cf. Ella Lonn, *Desertion During the Civil War* (1928), pp. v, 127 following.

2. Fortescue, *op. cit.*, vol. III, p. 254. In less than two weeks after the evacuation of Philadelphia, upward of 1,000 British deserters came into the patriot lines. *Writings of Washington*, vol. XII, pp. 129, 150.

3. Washington's comparison of other armies with his own is significant. *Writings of Washington*, vol. XXVI, p. 253.

4. Bolton, *op. cit.*, p. 127.


## ABSENTEEISM


5. Connecticut Historical Society *Collections*, vol. VII, pp. 17, 69; Massachusetts Historical Society *Proceedings*, vol. XV, p. 107.

6. *Writings of Washington*, vol. III, pp. 406, 441; Jonathan Burton's orderly book in Albert S. Batcheller (editor), *New Hampshire State Papers* (23 vols., 1874-1910), vol. XIV, pp. 676, 681.

7. *Writings of Washington*, vol. III, p. 346.

8. *Ibid.*, vol. IV, p. 128.

9. Greene's letter of Dec. 31, 1775, in Greene Papers.

10. *Writings of Washington*, vol. III, p. 367.

11. *Ibid.*, vol. IV, p. 2.

12. *Ibid.*, vol. V, p. 314.

13. *Journals of Congress*, vol. II, p. 333 (Nov. 7, 1775).

14. *Writings of Washington*, vol. V, p. 126; manuscript orderly book of the Rhode Island Regiment under Colonel Christopher Lippitt (Rhode Island Historical Society) under dates of Oct. 10 and Oct. 31, 1776.

15. *Writings of Washington*, vol. V, p. 126; John Morgan's circular letter of Nov. 4, 1776, in the John Warren Papers (Massachusetts Historical Society).

16. *Writings of Washington*, vol. VII, p. 417.

17. *Ibid.*, vol. IX, p. 342, and vol. XVII, p. 426.

18. *Ibid.*, vol. XVII, p. 426.

19. *Ibid.*, vol. V, p. 410, and vol. X, p. 189; Greene, *op. cit.*, vol. I, p. 187.

20. *Writings of Washington*, vol. VII, p. 219; *ibid.*, vol. XIII, pp. 96, 207.

21. *Ibid.*, vol. X, p. 153; *ibid.*, vol. XIII, p. 394.

22. *Ibid.*, vol. XIII, p. 145.

23. *Ibid.*, p. 394.

24. *Ibid.*, vol. XI, p. 226.

25. *Ibid.*, p. 228. In August, 1778, Colonel William Malcolm was taken to task for similar laxity. *Ibid.*, vol. XII, p. 372.

26. *Ibid.*, vol. XIII, p. 342; *ibid.*, vol. XXII, p. 123. See also Knox's leter in Isaac Q. Leake, *Memoir of the Life and Times of General John Lamb* (1850), p. 210. Examples of newspaper notices appear in *New Jersey Archives* (22 vols., 1880-1902), 2nd series, vol. I, p. 347, and *The Independent Chronicle and Universal Advertiser* for Feb. 23, 1777.

27. *Writings of Washington*, vol. VIII, p. 202.

28. *Ibid.*, vol. XXI, p. 179 (Feb. 3, 1781). He had been forbidding the practice on his own authority. *Ibid.*, vol. XI, p. 220, and vol. XXII, p. 128.

29. *Ibid.*, vol. XXII, p. 123.

30. *Ibid.*, vol. XXVI, p. 161.

31. Orders of Sept. 5, 1776, in Heath Papers.

32. Orders of Apr. 30 and Mar. 14, 1778, *ibid.*

33. Worthington C. Ford (editor), *General Orders Issued by Major-General William Heath* (1890), pp. 69, 73. In one case, however, an offender was cashiered although absent from his trial. Orders of Oct. 24, 1781, in Heath Papers.

34. For typical examples see Ichabod Goodwin's orderly book in Maine Historical Society *Collections*, 2nd series, vol. V (1894), p. 66;

Lieutenant Colonel Smith's manuscript orderly book (no. 17 in National Archives) under date of Sept. 17, 1778; and manuscript orderly book of Colonel Nathan Gallup's Regiment (Library of Congress) for Aug. 21, 1779.

35. E.g., manuscript orderly books of: John Pitman (Rhode Island Historical Society) for May 13, 1777, Moses Ashley (John Carter Brown Library) for Sept. 18, 1780, and Robert Walker (2 vols., in Library of Congress) for July 28, 1778.

36. Massachusetts Historical Society *Proceedings,* 2nd series, vol. VI, p. 102; Ebenezer Huntington's orderly book for Nov. 21, 1778, Apr. 5, 1780, and Apr. 17, 1783.

37. Orderly Book of the 2nd Massachusetts Regiment, May 25, 1779, Dec. 9, 1780, etc. Even this regiment frequently let men off with mild sentences. *Ibid.*, Mar. 17, 1780, June 21, 1781, etc. Cf. anonymous manuscript orderly book (no. 42 in National Archives) for Aug. 9, 1780.

38. Orderly Book of the 2nd Massachusetts Regiment, May 22, 1780, and Apr. 23, 1782.

39. Orderly Book kept at Gates' Headquarters (William L. Clements Library), Sept. 13, 1777; Bradish's orderly book for Oct. 22 and Nov. 2, 1778. Special leniency, on the other hand, was no more satisfactory. Lauber, *op. cit.*, p. 408.

40. *Charleston Yearbook* for 1889, pp. 156, 186.

41. Orderly Book of the First South Carolina Regiment in *South Carolina Historical and Genealogical Magazine* (vols. VII and VIII, 1906-1907), vol. VII, p. 132; *ibid.*, vol. VIII, pp. 25, 83.

42. Orderly Book at Siege of Savannah (Library of Congress), entries for Oct. 9, 1779, etc.

43. Charles Lee's orderly book for Apr. 1 and July 26, 1776.

44. Virginia Historical Society *Collections,* new series, vol. VI, p. 176; Charles Campbell (editor), *Orderly Book of that Portion of the Army Stationed at or near Williamsburg, Virginia* (1860), pp. 47, 55; Orderly Book of the Fourth Virginia Regiment (Library of Congress), June 10, 1776; Peter Muhlenberg's orderly book (Force Transcript in Library of Congress), June 21, 1781.

45. Steuben to Greene, Dec. 24, 1780, in Greene Papers.

46. Greene, *op. cit.*, vol. III, p. 85; Nathanael Greene's orderly book, Apr. 24 and June 21, 1781.

47. E.g., Thomas Thomas's manuscript orderly book (Library of Congress), Sept. 7, 1776. The *Writings of Washington* are full of this subject: e.g., vol. V, pp. 45, 337; vol. VIII, p. 328; and vol. XIII, p. 119.

48. Orderly Book of the 2nd Massachusetts Regiment, Sept. 27, 1777; *Pennsylvania Archives,* 6th series, vol. XIV, pp. 24, 36, 80.

49. William Coit's orderly book in Connecticut Historical Society *Collections,* vol. VII (1899), p. 69.

50. Fogg, *op. cit.,* Dec. 18, 1775.

51. *Writings of Washington,* vol. IX, p. 285; *ibid.,* vol. XII, pp. 111, 221; *ibid.,* vol. XVIII, pp. 466, 502; *ibid.,* vol. XXV, p. 225.

52. *Ibid.,* vol. XVIII, p. 73.

53. *Ibid.,* p. 503 (June 11, 1780).

54. *Ibid.,* p. 168.

55. *Ibid.,* vol. XI, p. 233; Palmer, *op cit.,* p. 156.

56. Charles Lee's orderly book, Apr. 30, 1776.

57. *Writings of Washington,* vol. IX, p. 125.

58. Richard Buckmaster's orderly book (Library of Congress), Oct. 23, 1778; *Writings of Washington,* vol. XII, p. 106.

## THE EXTENT OF DESERTION

1. Cf. Lonn, *op. cit.,* pp. 31, 144.

2. *Writings of Washington,* vol. IV, p. 431; *ibid.,* vol. VI, pp. 241, 320; *ibid.,* vol. XI, pp. 365, 406; Green Papers under dates of Mar. 8, 1780, Jan. 31, 1781, May 5, 1781, etc.

3. *American Historical Review,* vol. V, p. 715.

4. *Lafayette in Virginia,* p. 18 (July 1, 1781).

5. Sparks, *op. cit.,* vol. I, p. 417; Reed, *op. cit.,* vol. I, p. 194.

6. Force, *op. cit.,* 5th series, vol. I, pp. 370, 470; *St. Clair Papers,* vol. I, p. 437.

7. Sumter to Marion (June 7, 1781) and to Greene (June 19, 1781) in Greene Papers.

8. Marion to Greene, July 24 and Sept. 27, 1781, *ibid.;* Marion to Gates, Nov. 22, 1780, *ibid.*

9. Gibbes, *op. cit.,* vol. I, p. 243; *Public Papers of George Clinton,* vol. I, pp. 503-504, 522.

10. Sparks, *op. cit.*, vol. I, pp. 280, 329.

11. The status of militia prisoners was particularly uncertain in the South after 1780. Marion to Greene, June 16, 1782, Greene Papers in Library of Congress.

12. *Illinois Historical Collections*, vol. VIII, pp. xxxiv, 596; *Calendar of Virginia State Papers*, vol. II, p. 265.

13. Marion to Greene, Jan. 14 and May 6, 1781, in Greene Papers; Greene to Huntington (Jan. 31, 1781) and to Congress (Apr. 22, 1781), *ibid.*

14. *Writings of Washington*, vol. V, p. 451; *ibid.*, vol. XIII, p. 237.

15. *Ibid.*, vol. XII, p. 237.

16. Tower, *op. cit.*, vol. I, p. 487.

17. *Writings of Washington*, vol. XII, p. 368; Bradish's orderly book, Aug. 25, 1778.

18. *Writings of Washington*, vol. VI, p. 4.

19. *Ibid.*, pp. 96, 371. Philip Schuyler was having a similar experience in the North. Force, *op. cit.*, 5th series, vol. II, p. 1299.

20. *Writings of Washington*, vol. VI, p. 402.

21. *Ibid.*, vol. VII, pp. 33, 45, 253.

22. *Calendar of Virginia State Papers*, vol. I, p. 603; John Piper's orderly book (Library of Congress), Apr. 10, 1781.

23. Reed, *op. cit.*, vol. II, p. 345; Sparks, *op. cit.*, vol. III, p. 109.

24. Hamilton, *op. cit.*, vol. I, p. 149.

25. Greene to Nash, Mar. 6, 1781, in Greene Papers.

26. Greene to Jefferson, Mar. 10, 1781, *ibid.* A month earlier he had had only 180 men. Greene to John Butler, Feb. 12, and 13, 1781, *ibid.*

27. Kapp, *Life of Kalb*, p. 138.

28. For other examples of mass desertion see *Writings of Washington*, vol. IV, pp. 137 ff.; *ibid.*, vol. VI, pp. 14, 234, 312; Greene Papers under dates of May 6 and 11, 1781, July 20, 1782, etc.

29. Orders of May 21, 1777, in Heath Papers.

30. *Writings of Washington*, vol. XI, p. 139.

31. Steuben's letter of May 15, 1781, in Kapp, *Life of Steuben*, p. 429.

32. *Archives of Maryland*, vol. XLV, p. 183; *ibid.*, vol. XLVII, pp. 306, 426, 458, 485.

33. Dr. John Morgan to Dr. John Warren, Nov. 7, 1776, in Warren Papers.

34. *Writings of Washington,* vol. VII, p. 30.

35. *Ibid.,* vol. XXIV, p. 38 (Mar. 1, 1782).

36. Pickering, *op. cit.,* vol. I, p. 162; orders of Nov. 23, 1777, in Heath Papers.

37. *Calendar of Virginia State Papers,* vol. I, p. 554; Greene to Lincoln, June 18, 1783, in Greene Papers.

38. At High Hills of Santee, Aug. 1, 1781, in Greene Papers.

39. The figure 3000 given by Lecky and Fisher is apparently based on a report by Joseph Galloway, a Loyalist. Lecky, *op. cit.,* vol. IV, p. 63; Fisher, *op. cit.,* vol. II, p. 123; Stevens, *op. cit.,* no. 2094. Van Tyne's estimate of 2300 seems more reasonable. Van Tyne, *American Revolution,* p. 237.

40. *Massachusetts Soldiers and Sailors of the Revolutionary War* (17 vols., 1896-1908), passim.

41. *Archives of Maryland,* vol. XVIII, pp. 78-260, 273-292.

42. Some officers appear as repeated deserters. Numbers of recruits deserted the day after enlistment, and some left on the very day when they joined. O'Callaghan, *op. cit.,* vol. XV, pp. 174-244.

## THE CAUSES OF DESERTION

1. Above, p. 107.

2. Bouton, *op. cit.,* vol. VII, p. 460; Force, *op. cit.,* 4th series, vol. II, p. 1080.

3. *Writings of Washington,* vol. VI, p. 238.

4. *Ibid.,* vol. VIII, pp. 8, 17, 161, 128.

5. Stedman, *op. cit.,* vol. I, p. 310. Galloway's statement lists only 283 natives among 1134 such deserters. Stevens, *op. cit.,* no. 2094.

6. Massachusetts Historical Society *Proceedings,* 2nd series, vol. VI, p. 95; James Livingston to Greene, Oct. 11, 1780, in Greene Papers. Cf. above, pp. 14-15.

7. *Writings of Washington,* vol. XIV, p. 349, and vol. XXIV, p. 401. Deserters from the Saratoga prisoners who enlisted in the patriot army almost invariably deserted. Maine Historical Society *Collections,* 2nd series, vol. V, pp. 53, 61. Greene believed that a third of the British force in

the South in 1781 consisted of deserters and prisoners from the American army. Greene to Congress, May 10, 1781, in Greene Papers.

8. Marion to Greene, Sept. 29, 1782, *ibid.*

9. John Laurens to Greene, Mar. 18, 1782, *ibid.*

10. He added that physical standards were high. It must be recalled, of course, that in 1782 the need for troops was not pressing. *Providence Gazette*, Mar. 16, 1782.

11. Force, *op. cit.*, 5th series, vol. I, p. 1217. Cf. *ibid.*, vol. III, p. 1301.

12. Greene, *op. cit.*, vol. II, p. 135; Smallwood to Washington, Jan. 26, 1778, in Washington Papers.

13. *Writings of Washington*, vol. XIV, p. 257.

14. *Ibid.*, vol. XVI, p. 384; *ibid.*, vol. XVII, pp. 134, 207.

15. Sparks, *op. cit.*, vol. III, p. 265; Tower, *op. cit.*, vol. II, p. 259.

16. *Writings of Washington*, vol. III, p. 316.

17. *Ibid.*, vol. VII, p. 111.

18. *Ibid.*, vol. VIII, p. 111.

19. *Ibid.*, vol. XV, p. 252.

20. Orderly books cited below, pp. 135-141.

21. William Davies to Greene, Apr. 16, 1781, in Greene Papers.

22. Muhlenberg, *op. cit.*, p. 415.

23. *Writings of Washington*, vol. VII, p. 480.

24. *Ibid.*, vol. VIII, pp. 8, 123.

25. *Ibid.*, p. 198; *St. Clair Papers*, vol. I, p. 523.

26. Hall, *op. cit.*, p. 240; *Writings of Washington*, vol. XVIII, p. 30.

27. Van Tyne, *American Revolution*, p. 305.

28. *Writings of Washington*, vol. XXIV, p. 289.

29. Thomas Posey to Greene, Feb. 22, 1782, in Greene Papers; Charles Lynch's letter of Apr. 2, 1781, *ibid.* Throughout the country privateering lured many men from the army. A return of deserters from Colonel Alexander Scammell's New Hampshire Regiment (June 17, 1779) in the Charles P. Greenough Papers (Massachusetts Historical Society) indicates that out of 44 deserters whose whereabouts was known, 19 were engaged in privateering.

30. Force, *op. cit.*, 5th series, vol. I, p. 827; Reed, *op. cit.*, vol. I, p. 215.

31. Letters of Feb. 8 and May 4, 1778, in Stillé, *op. cit.*, pp. 118, 120. Nine out of ten deaths and desertions, Wayne insisted, were due to dirt and nakedness. *Ibid.*, p. 125.

32. Henry, *op. cit.*, vol. III, p. 232; Marion to Greene, Jan. 1 and Mar. 13, 1782, in Greene Papers.

33. Greene to Jefferson, Dec. 14, 1780, Greene Papers.

34. *Public Papers of George Clinton*, vol. I, pp. 487, 490, 494, 502.

35. *Ibid.*, vol. V, p. 421; Massachusetts Historical Society *Collections*, 7th series, vol. IV, p. 334.

36. *Writings of Washington*, vol. XX, p. 35.

37. *Ibid.*, vol. IV, p. 147.

38. Pickering, *op. cit.*, vol. I, p. 203.

39. *Writings of Washington*, vol. XVII, pp. 293, 432.

40. *Ibid.*, vol. XXIV, pp. 289, 440; Marion to Greene, Jan. 1 and Mar. 13, 1782, in Greene Papers.

## THE PREVENTION OF DESERTION

1. Connecticut Historical Society *Collections*, vol. XX, p. 301; Maine Historical Society *Collections*, 2nd series, vol. V, pp. 53, 61.

2. *Pennsylvania Archives*, 2nd series, vol. XI, p. 564. Washington had to urge officers not to countenance enlistment from one corps into another. *Writings of Washington*, vol. V, p. 327.

3. *Writings of Washington*, vol. X, pp. 172, 519.

4. *Ibid.*, vol. VII, pp. 246, 251.

5. *Ibid.*, vol. XXI, p. 175; *ibid.*, vol. XXIV, p. 61.

6. *Writings of Washington*, vol. XIX, p. 374, and vol. XXI, p. 201.

7. As examples of many such orders, see *ibid.*, vol. VIII, p. 64; *ibid.*, vol. IX, p. 243, and *Charleston Yearbook* (1889), p. 166.

8. *Writings of Washington*, vol. VIII, p. 106.

9. *Ibid.*, p. 230, and vol. XXIII, p. 94. George Rogers Clark camped on the island at the falls of the Ohio in 1778 in the hope that the location would prevent desertion, but some of his men left none the less. *Illinois Historical Collections*, vol. VIII, p. x.

10. Steuben's "Plan for Preventing Desertion," Dec. 24, 1780, in Greene Papers. Steuben said that he had presented the plan to Governor Thomas Jefferson.

11. Above, p. 65.

12. *Writings of Washington,* vol. XXI, p. 180.

13. *Ibid.,* vol. XVII, p. 253; *ibid.,* vol. XVIII, pp. 401, 450; *ibid.,* vol. XXIV, p. 340.

14. The difficulty, if not impossibility, of securing adequate lists of deserters illustrates this remissness. *Pennsylvania Archives,* 2nd series, vol. XI, p. 475; anonymous manuscript orderly book (no. 7 in Boston Public Library), May 12, 1782.

15. *Writings of Washington,* vol. XII, p. 530; *ibid.,* vol. XV, pp. 402, 444.

16. Orders of Sept. 4, 1776, in Heath Papers.

17. The prisoners got through the chain of sentries into the town, and their women strolled in the streets of Cambridge. Orders of Nov. 9, 1777, Dec. 20, 1777, etc., *ibid.*

18. Orders of Jan. 6, 1782, *ibid.*

19. Delaware Historical Society *Papers,* vol. LVI, p. 127; Massachusetts Historical Society *Proceedings,* 2nd series, vol. III, p. 129.

20. *Writings of Washington,* vol. XII, p. 497; *ibid.,* vol. XVIII, p. 389.

21. *Ibid.,* vol. X, p. 421.

22. *Ibid.,* vol. XI, p. 250.

23. *Ibid.,* vol. XIV, pp. 403, 427.

24. *Ibid., vol.* III, pp. 406, 441.

25. *Ibid.,* vol. V, p. 499; *ibid.,* vol. XVIII, p. 401; *ibid.,* vol. XXIV, pp. 340, 447; Greene, *op. cit.,* vol. II, p. 217; John Sevier to Greene, Nov. 9, 1781, in Greene Papers.

26. Ford, *op. cit.,* pp. 39-40, 42; Frederick Cook (editor), *Journals of the Military Expedition of Major General John Sullivan against the Six Nations of Indians in 1779* (1887), pp. 252-253, 277.

27. *Writings of Washington,* vol. VIII, p. 440; *Journals of Congress,* vol. VIII, p. 593.

28. *Writings of Washington,* vol. X, pp. 254-255; *ibid.,* vol. XXIV, p. 321.

29. *Archives of Maryland,* vol. XLIII, p. 330; *ibid.,* vol. XLV, pp. 27, 62.

30. Bolton, *op. cit.,* p. 172.

31. Stark, *op. cit.,* p. 113.

32. *Writings of Washington*, vol. III, p. 406; *ibid.*, vol. V, p. 293.

33. *Lee Papers*, vol. II, p. 35.

34. *Public Records of the Colony of Connecticut*, vol. XV, p. 370.

35. *Writings of Washington*, vol. VII, p. 81.

36. *Ibid.*, p. 82.

37. *Ibid.*, p. 191.

38. Persons unable to pay were to be flogged. *Journals of Congress*, vol. III, p. 324.

39. *Ibid.*, vol. V, p. 831.

40. *Journals of Congress*, vol. III, p. 325 (Nov. 4, 1775).

41. *Ibid.*, vol. VII, pp. 108, 115-118 (Feb. 12-13, 1777), 154-155 (Feb. 25, 1777).

42. *Ibid.*, vol. IX, p. 813; *Writings of Washington*, vol. IX, pp. 442, 492.

43. *Journals of Congress*, vol. IX, p. 813.

44. *Ibid.*, vol. XIV, p. 663 (May 23, 1779).

45. *Writings of Washington*, vol. XVI, p. 360; Roberts' orderly book, Sept. 9, 1776.

46. Orders of Nov. 23, 1777, in Heath Papers.

47. *Laws of New Hampshire*, vol. IV, pp. 92-94, 734; John R. Bartlett (editor), *Records of the Colony of Rhode Island and Providence Plantations in New England* (10 vols., 1856-1865), vol. VII, p. 353; *ibid.*, vol. VIII, pp. 143, 640; *Public Records of the Colony of Connecticut*, vol. XV, p. 196; A. C. Goodell and others (editors), *The Acts and Resolves, Public and Private of the Province of Massachusetts Bay* (21 vols., 1869-1922), vol. XIX, pp. 557, 625; *Laws of New York*, vol. I, 397; *Acts of the General Assembly of the State of New Jersey* (4 vols., 1778-1782), vol. III, p. 122; *Statutes at Large of Pennsylvania*, vol. IX, pp. 59-63, 218; *Laws of the State of Delaware* (2 vols., 1797), vol. II, p. 625; *Laws of Maryland* (3 vols., 1777-1783), vol. I, chapters XXI and XLIII; Hening, *op. cit.*, vol. IX, pp. 91, 289, 344; *North Carolina Records*, vol. X, p. 641; *ibid.*, vol. XXIV, pp. 157 following; *Statutes at Large of South Carolina*, vol. IV, pp. 340, 412, 514; Robert Watkins and George Watkins (editors), *Digest of the Laws of the State of Georgia* (1800), p. 202.

48. E.g., *Laws of New Hampshire*, vol. IV, pp. 474, 502; *Statutes of Pennsylvania*, vol. XI, p. 578. A Pennsylvania law in 1780 provided a

heavy fine or one year's imprisonment for ship officers who knowingly employed deserters on armed vessels. *Ibid.*, vol. X, p. 222.

49. *New England Chronicle or Essex Gazette,* June 22 and 29, 1775.

50. No reward was offered in some of the earliest. *Ibid.*, June 2 to Aug. 3, 1775. The rewards increased as time went on. *Ibid.*, Aug. 10, 1775; *Pennsylvania Ledger,* Feb. 3 and 17, 1776.

51. *Virginia Gazettee,* Dec. 9, 1780.

52. *Ibid.*, Mar. 25 and other dates in 1780.

53. E.g., *Providence Gazette,* July 6 and 13, 1776.

54. *Ibid.*, July 6 and 13, 1776; *Pennsylvania Ledger,* Feb. 3 and 17, 1776.

55. *New Jersey Archives,* 2nd series, vol. II, p. 197; *ibid.*, vol. III, p. 523.

56. The *Providence Gazette,* e.g., carried several in 1776, a few in 1777, and a large number in 1781. Cf. *Massachusetts Spy,* 1775-1777, passim.

57. E.g., James Sullivan (editor), *Minutes of the Albany Committee of Correspondence, 1775-1778* (2 vols., 1923-1925), vol. I, pp. 441, 489; *Minutes of the Provincial Congress and the Council of Safety of the State of New Jersey, 1775-1776* (1879), pp. 199, 200, 207.

Some Maryland counties had poor jails or none at all, and deserters held there often escaped. *Archives of Maryland,* vol. XLV, p. 33; *ibid.*, vol. XLVII, pp. 118, 196.

58. *Writings of Washington,* vol. XVIII, p. 462; *ibid.*, vol. XXIV, p. 493; *Journals of Congress,* vol. IX, p. 816; above, pp. 91-92.

59. *Archives of Maryland,* vol. XLV, p. 68 (Aug. 30, 1780).

60. Sparks, *op. cit.*, vol. II, p. 77 (Feb. 21, 1778).

61. Hall, *op. cit.*, p. 240.

62. *Archives of Maryland,* vol. XLV, p. 548, and vol. XLVII, p. 468.

63. Sparks, *op. cit.*, vol. I, p. 362; Eckenrode, *op. cit.*, pp. 247-250.

64. Nathaniel Pendleton to Greene, July 17, 1783, in Greene Papers.

65. Council journals for Jan. 16, 1777, in *North Carolina Records,* vol. XXII, p. 908. The governor's proclamation was issued on Jan. 25, 1777. *Ibid.*, p. 903.

66. *Journals of Congress,* vol. X, p. 163 (Feb. 13, 1778).

67. Greene to George Baylor, May 27, 1783, in Greene Papers.

68. *North Carolina Records,* vol. XVI, pp. 516, 627; Greene to Sumner, July 19, 1781, in Greene Papers.

69. *North Carolina Records,* vol. XVI, p. 63.

70. Thomas Burke to Greene, Mar. 28, 1782, in Greene Papers; *Illinois Historical Collections,* vol. VIII, p. 29.

71. *Writings of Washington,* vol. XV, p. 134 (May 23, 1779).

72. *Illinois Historical Collections,* vol. VIII, p. 116 (Nov. 19, 1779).

73. Proclamation of June 19, 1779, *ibid.,* p. 343; letter of May 11, 1780, *ibid.,* p. 418.

74. Hand to Gates, Apr. 21, 1778, in Hand Correspondence; Hand to Washington, Ft. Pitt, Nov. 9, 1777, in Washington Papers.

75. Sparks, *op. cit.,* vol. III, p. 21 (July 15, 1780).

76. Hand Correspondence, 1781.

77. *Writings of Washington,* vol. XXII, p. 354, and vol. XXVI, p. 123.

78. *Ibid.,* vol. XVIII, p. 311 (Apr. 28, 1780).

79. *Journals of Congress,* vol. II, p. 113 following; *ibid.,* vol. III, p. 332, and vol. V, p. 792.

80. Typical examples appear in Benjamin Craft's journal in Eessex Institute *Historical Collections,* vol. III, pp. 57, 168, 169; and in Nathaniel Morgan's journal in Connecticut Historical Society *Collections,* vol. VII, pp. 101, 105.

Floggings up to 78 lashes were given at times by means of two sentences, one for desertion and one for reenlistment. Gates' orderly book, Aug. 24 and Sept. 1, 1776. Fines and imprisonment or drumming out of the army, etc., were often administered in addition to the floggings. *Ibid.,* Sept. 1 and 6, 1776, and Oct. 3, 1776; *Writings of Washington,* vol. III, p. 339, and vol. IV, pp. 268, 342.

81. Montgomery's orderly book, July 17, 1775.

82. Philip Schuyler's manuscript orderly book (Library of Congress), Oct. 11, 1775.

83. *Writings of Washington,* vol. VI, pp. 114, 122.

84. Schuyler's orderly book, Sept. 4, 1776; Orderly Book of the 2nd Massachusetts Regiment, Sept. 28, 1777.

85. Gates' orderly book, Sept. 4 and Nov. 3, 1776; manuscript orderly book (no. 58 in National Archives), Apr. 22, 1782; many other examples in *Writings of Washington,* passim.

86. *Journals of Congress,* vol. VI, p. 933.

87. Robert Howe's orders of Nov. 17, 1780, in Henry Whiting (editor), *Revolutionary Orders of General Washington* (1844), p. 138.

88. *Writings of Washington,* vol. XV, p. 49.

89. John Laurance to Washington, Feb. 5, 1778, in Washington Papers.

90. *Writings of Washington,* vol. VII, p. 353; *ibid.,* vol. VIII, p. 50, and vol. IX, p. 80.

91. *Ibid.,* vol. XV, pp. 388, 399.

92. *Ibid.,* vol. VI, p. 181, and vol. XXIII, pp. 96, 171; above, pp. 90-91.

93. *Ibid.,* vol. XIII, pp. 55, 60, 95; *ibid.,* vol. XXIV, pp. 325, 328.

94. Stephen Kemble's orderly book in New York Historical Society *Collections,* vol. XVI, pp. 483, 517, 582, etc.

95. To be sure, the British problem was greatest among the Hessians, who were leniently treated. But the mercenary motives of hired troops must be considered.

96. Orderly books already cited contain many examples. See also Worthington C. Ford (editor), *General Orders Issued by Major-General William Heath* (1890), pp. 12, 22, 56, 108.

97. For actual executions see *ibid.,* p. 78; Edward W. Hocker, *The Fighting Parson of the American Revolution: A Biography of General Peter Muhlenberg* (1936), p. 116.

98. *North Carolina Records,* vol. XV, p. 530 (July 14, 1781).

99. Above, pp. 71-72, 75-76.

## LENIENCY TOWARD DESERTION

1. Of a total of some 1250 penalties for desertion, chosen at random for special study, almost exactly two-thirds were floggings. Orderly books already cited; John Burnham's manuscript orderly book (Library of Congress), Feb. 4, 1777.

2. Service on a Continental frigate for the rest of one's term or for

the duration of the war was not uncommon. *Writings of Washington*, vol. VIII, pp. 269, 401-405; *ibid.*, vol. IX, pp. 168, 179. Running the gauntlet, although not provided for in the Articles of War, was sometimes substituted for a regular flogging with the cat-o'-nine-tails or with rods. Lauber, *op. cit.*, pp. 411, 587. Confinement for a year or so, or even for the rest of the war, was used in a few instances. Robert Kirkwood's orderly book in Joseph B. Turner (editor), Delaware Historical Society *Papers*, vol. LVI (1910), p. 83; *Writings of Washington*, vol. XVII, pp. 65-66.

3. One hundred lashes for each of several offenses—such as desertion, reenlistment, and changing one's name—might bring the total to 300 or even 500. *Writings of Washington*, vol. XI, pp. 266, 487; Samuel Elbert's orderly book in Georgia Historical Society *Collections*, vol. V, part 2 (1902), p. 182; Cook, *op. cit.*, p. 21.

4. Hall, *op. cit.*, p. 214; *The Order Book of Captain Leonard Bleeker* (1865), p. 85.

5. Typical of a host of instances are: "The Orders of Mercer, Sullivan, and Stirling," *American Historical Review*, vol. III (1897), p. 306; *Writings of Washington*, vol. V, p. 313, and vol. VIII, pp. 435-436.

6. *Writings of Washington*, vol. IX, pp. 439, 492, and passim.

7. *Ibid.*, vol. VIII, pp. 213-214, and vol. XXIII, pp. 320 following; Orderly Book oi the 2nd Massachusetts Regiment, Feb. 15, 1780; Cook, *op. cit.*, pp. 253-254.

8. In the later years the States usually asked Washington to issue their proclamations. Examples of State proclamations appear in *New Jersey Archives*, 2nd series, vol. I, p. 5, and Hening, *op. cit.*, vol. X, p. 265.

9. E.g., *Writings of Washington*, vol. IX, p. 165, and vol. XVIII, pp. 281, 287.

10. *Ibid.*, vol. VII, p. 364.

11. *Ibid.*, vol. IX, pp. 426, 496; *Journals of Congress*, vol. IX, p. 816 (Oct. 17, 1777).

12. Proclamations of Mar. 10 and Apr. 22, 1779, in *Writings of Washington*, vol. XIV, pp. 222, 429 following. Examples of newspaper advertisements of such proclamations appear in *Pennsylvania Gazette and Weekly Advertiser*, Mar. 24 and June 16, 1779.

13. It was probably dated Feb. 8, 1782. *Providence Gazette*, Mar. 16, 1782; *Writings of Washington*, vol. XXIII, p. 469.

14. Less than a dozen are mentioned in ***Writings of Washington:*** e.g., vol. VIII, pp. 177, 343, 361. Cf. orders of Jan. 9, 1778, in Heath Papers.

15. ***North Carolina Records.*** vol. XI, p. 522; Sumter to Greene, Nov. 24, 1781, in Greene Papers.

16. ***Writings of Washington,*** vol. XVI, pp. 422 following (Oct. 9, 1779).

17. ***Ibid.,*** vol. IX, p. 407.

18. ***Ibid.,*** vol. XVIII, p. 236.

19. ***Ibid.,*** vol. XXI, p. 308 (Feb. 27, 1781).

20. ***Ibid.,*** vol. XXIII, pp. 456, 469.

21. Delaware Historical Society ***Papers,*** vol. LVI, p. 78; ***Charleston Yearbook*** (1889), p. 258.

## *REFERENCES*

# *IV: The Maintenance of Morale*

### REWARDS, RECREATION AND REGALIA

1. E. g., *Secret Journals of the Acts and Proceedings of Congress* (4 vols., 1821), vol. I, p. 28; *Rhode Island Colonial Records,* vol. VIII, p. 186. The medals and trophies were for officers. Actual bestowal often occurred only after long delay. *Journals of Congress,* vol. VIII, pp. 579, 580; *ibid.,* vol. XXI, pp. 1080-1085.

2. *Writings of Washington,* vol. XIII, p. 422, and vol. XVII, p. 80; Pettit to Greene, Mar. 15, 1782, in Greene Papers.

3. *Journals of Congress,* vol. IV, pp. 78, 89; *ibid.,* vol. VII, p. 79, etc.; Kapp, *Life of Kalb,* pp. 238, 326.

4. Hamilton, *op. cit.,* vol. I, p. 168. Officers' widows suffered, and official expenses were not properly provided for. Burnett, *op. cit.,* vol. II, p. 378; *ibid.,* vol. V, p. 275.

5. *Writings of Washington,* vol. XV, p. 252; Hening, *op. cit.,* vol. X, p. 465.

6. *The Military Journal of George Ewing* (1928), Apr. 15, 1778.

7. *Writings of Washington,* vol. XVIII, p. 261; Fitzpatrick, *George Washington Himself,* p. 369.

8. Pickering, *op. cit.,* vol. I, pp. 399, 400.

9. *Writings of Washington,* vol. IV, p. 347; *ibid.,* vol. V, p. 367, and vol. VIII, pp. 129, 152; William Young's journal in *Pennsylvania Magazine,* vol. VIII (1884), pp. 267, 272.

10. Summer sports were considered unhealthful. Orderly Book of the 4th Virginia Regiment, June 9 and 24, 1776; manuscript orderly book (no. 14 in National Archives), July 18, 1776.

11. *Writings of Washington,* vol. VIII, p. 29. Washington had some

appreciation of outdoor games. *Ibid.*, p. 129. There was a good deal of informal recreation such as games of ball, shinny, dancing, hunting, and fishing. *Pennsylvania Archives,* 2nd series, vol. XI, pp. 682-706.

12. John C. Miller, *Sam Adams; Pioneer in Propaganda* (1936), pp. 61, 112, 140, 190; Ewing, *op. cit.*, pp. 44-46.

13. George H. Preble, *History of the Flag of the United States of America* (1880), pp. 195 following.

14. *Ibid.*, p. 277.

15. *Writings of Washington,* vol. XII, p. 389, and vol. XXIII, p. 181.

16. *Ibid.*, vol. XXIV, p. 454.

17. *Ibid.*, vol. III, pp. 456, 473, etc.; *Charleston Yearbook* (1889), p. 241; Bolton, *op. cit.*, p. 155.

18. John C. Fitzpatrick, *The Spirit of the Revolution* (1924), p. 175; Aaron Wright's journal in *Historical Magazine,* 1st series, vol. VI (1862), p. 211.

19. *Writings of Washington,* vol. XIII, p. 440, and vol. XIV, p. 110.

20. Moses C. Tyler, *Literary History of the American Revolution* (2 vols., 1897), vol. II, pp. 170-173, 180 following.

21. *Writings of Washington,* vol. IV, p. 155, and vol. VII, p. 452.

22. *Ibid.*, vol. VII, p. 422, and vol. XXV, p. 402; Fitzpatrick, *Spirit of the Revolution,* pp. 117, 133, 137. There is no doubt but that the ragged condition of many soldiers was a serious detriment to self-respect, discipline, and morale.

23. *Writings of Washington,* vol. III, p. 339, 404, etc.; William L. Calver, "Researches into the American Army Button of the Revolutionary War," *Journal of the American Military Foundation,* vol. I (1937), p. 151.

24. Reed, *op. cit.*, vol. II, p. 130.

25. Stillé, *op. cit.*, p. 24.

26. *Writings of Washington,* vol. XXIV, pp. 487-488, and vol. XXV, p. 7. A board of officers passed on all candidates. *Ibid.*, vol. XXV, pp. 481-482. The Purple Heart was apparently awarded to only three men during the Revolution. Fitzpatrick, *Spirit of the Revolution,* p. 190; Howard M. Chapin, *Notes on the Badge of Merit of 1782* (1925), pp. 4-6.

## PROPAGANDA

1. The officers' use of propaganda is discussed above, pp. 99-102.

2. Edward F. Humphrey, *Nationalism and Religion in America,*

*1774-1789* (1924), p. 4; Alice M. Baldwin, *The New England Clergy and the American Revolution* (1928), passim.

3. Claude H. Van Tyne, *England and America* (1927), pp. 77-79.

4. *Journals of Congress*, vol. II, p. 220; *ibid.*, vol. V, pp. 192, 198, etc.

5. *Charleston Yearbook* (1889), pp. 170-172; *Writings of Washington*, vol. VIII, pp. 138, 203.

6. Most of the journals and orderly books already cited are full of references to divine service twice on Sunday and (for New England corps) to week-day morning and evening prayers. See also Paul Lunt's journal in Samuel A. Greene (editor), *American History Pamphlets*, vol. II (1872), pp. 14-15; Noah Chapin's journal (typewritten copy in Library of Boston Athenaeum), July 2, 1775.

7. Kirkland, *op. cit.*, pp. 13-14; Parkman's journal, passim.

8. *Writings of Washington*, vol. XI, pp. 78, 342.

9. Ebenezer David's letter of Aug. 31, 1776, in David Letters, John Carter Brown Library.

10. Joel T. Headley, *The Chaplains and Clergy of the Revolution* (1864), pp. 68-73.

11. Hocker, *op. cit.*, pp. 50 following; Baldwin, *op. cit.*, p. 164.

12. Baldwin, *op. cit.*, p. 164.

13. Theodore A. Zunder, *The Early Days of Joel Barlow, a Connecticut Wit* (1934), pp. 99-105, 114, 117.

14. Van Tyne, *Loyalists in the American Revolution*, pp. 198-202.

15. Force, *op. cit.*, 5th series, vol. III, p. 576; *Writings of Washington*, vol. VI, p. 15.

16. *Writings of Washington*, vol. VIII, p. 117, and vol. X, pp. 82, 104.

17. *Ibid.*, vol. XXI, pp. 376, 402; Greene to William Henderson (Aug. 12, 1781) and to Washington (Aug. 26, 1781) in Greene Papers.

18. William Duer to Greene, Feb. 28, 1780, in Greene Papers; Edward Bangs (editor), *Journal of Lieutenant Isaac Bangs* (1890), p. 49.

19. Burnett, *op. cit.*, vol. IV, p. 322. Officers mocked at "the subtlety of this system of lies told by everybody and believed by no one." Kapp, *Life of Kalb*, p. 177.

20. *Writings of Washington*, vol. IV, pp. 87, 312-313; *ibid.*, vol.

XIV, pp. 165, 294; *Journals of Congress,* vol. XII, p. 1101.

21. See the *Massachusetts Spy,* Dec. 29, 1775, for an example of valuable news. As to officers' use of newspapers, see *Writings of Washington,* vol. VIII, pp. 158, 240.

22. *Writings of Washington,* vol. III, p. 332, and vol. V, p. 109; Stark, *op. cit.,* p. 132.

23. *Writings of Washington,* vol. X, p. 437.

24. *Ibid.,* vol. XXI, p. 185, and vol. XXV, p. 176; Tyler, *op. cit.,* vol. II, pp. 36-38.

25. *Writings of Washington,* vol. VIII, p. 443.

26. *Journals of Congress,* vol. IV, p. 173; *Secret Journals of Congress,* vol. I, pp. 41 following; Burnett, *op. cit.,* vol. I, p. 474, and vol. II, pp. 13-14, 59.

27. *Journals of Congress,* vol. X, p. 20 (Jan. 5, 1778); *Writings of Washington,* vol. VIII, p. 445.

28. Greene, *op. cit.,* vol. III, p. 296.

29. Greene to Walters, July 10, 1781, in Greene Papers.

30. Greene to Congress, July 17, 1781, *ibid.*

31. *Lafayette in Virginia,* p. 34 (July 27, 1781).

32. Parkman's journal, Aug. 6, 1780, and Feb. 11, 1781; Massachusetts Historical Society *Collections,* 6th series, vol. IX, p. 400.

33. E.g., William Henshaw to Mrs. Phoebe Henshaw, Apr. 28, 1775, in Henshaw Papers (Library of American Antiquarian Society); Simms, *op. cit.,* p. 110.

34. *Writings of Washington,* vol. III, pp. 294 following, and passim.

35. The *Journals of Congress* indicate that Congress appointed no less than fourteen such days. The States co-operated, and also appointed days of their own. See, e.g., *Pennsylvania Colonial Records* (16 vols., 1838-1853), vol. XI, pp. 369, 627; *North Carolina Records,* vol. XII, p. 34.

36. Greene, *op. cit.,* vol. I, p. 122; *Writings of Washington,* vol. IV, p. 321.

37. *Journals of Congress,* vol. V, pp. 510-516; Fitzpatrick, *Spirit of the Revolution,* pp. 11, 26.

38. *Works of John Adams,* vol. IX, p. 420; Force, *op. cit.,* 5th series, vol. I, pp. 119, 205, 227.

39. Simms, *op cit.,* pp. 159, 165; *Writings of Washington,* vol. V, p. 469, and passim.

40. *Writings of Washington*, vol. III, pp. 224, 245; Fred L. Pattee (editor), *The Poems of Philip Freneau, Poet of the American Revolution* (3 vols., 1902-1907), vol. I, passim.

41. Van Tyne, *Loyalists in the American Revolution*, pp. 217-219; *Writings of Washington*, vol. XVIII, pp. 238, 445.

42. Reed, *op. cit.*, vol. II, p. 316; *Writings of Washington*, vol. XI, pp. 275, 299, 450.

43. Van Tyne, *War of Independence*, pp. 6, 403-404; *Journals of Congress*, vol. II, pp. 128-157. The British were called "diabolical contrivers" of "Persecution and Imprisonment, scorn and Insult, Blocks, Halters, Gibbets," intent on leaving America in ruins with "homes turned into barracks and bawdy-houses for Hessians." George III was pictured as more vile than Cain or Herod. The meanness of British officers "would mark a Savage with Eternal Infamy." The Loyalist were "poor dogs," an "infernal crew," "obnoxious vermin," incarnate "ghosts from hell"!

44. Hall, *op. cit.*, pp. 255, 257; Tower, *op. cit.*, vol. II, pp. 301-303.

45. Sparks, *op. cit.*, vol. III, pp. 403, 423; Tower, *op. cit.*, vol. II, p. 229.

46. Pattee, *op. cit.*, vol. II, p. 86; Van Tyne, *American Revolution*, pp. 61, 71 following.

47. Trumbull, *op. cit.*, pp. 34-36; Bolton, *op. cit.*, p. 186.

48. *Writings of Washington*, vol. IX, p. 160.

49. Many examples appear in *Journals of Congress:* e.g., vol. XII, pp. 987, 1062, 1125-1129. As to plans for systematic works, see Burnett, *op. cit.*, vol. I, p. 143, and *Warren-Adams Letters*, vol. I, p. 143. Benjamin Franklin planned the school book, which was to have included 35 pictures. Albert H. Smyth (editor), *The Writings of Benjamin Franklin* (10 vols., pp. 1905-1907), vol. VIII, p. 7 (Feb. 2, 1780).

50. Soldiers often recorded their hatred of England. E. g., Fleet Green's manuscript journal (typewritten copy in Library of Rhode Island Historical Society), passim.

51. Many examples appear in *Writings of Washington.* Very rarely was a maritime success noticed, possibly because the lure of privateering was so strong. A good example of the effectiveness of a speech appears in Smith, *Our Struggle for the Fourteenth Colony*, vol. I, pp. 576-577.

52. Ebenezer Sprout's orderly book (manuscript copy in Library of Congress), Jan. 13, 1780.

53. Piper's orderly book, Mar. 26, 1781.

54. Ford, *General Orders Issued by Major General Israel Putnam*, pp. 83-84.

55. E.g., William Smallwood's manuscript orderly book (Library of Congress), July 26, 1780; Nathanael Greene's orderly book, Nov. 7 and 12, 1780.

56. Consult works already cited dealing with the officers named; also Joseph Bowman's journal in *Illinois Historical Collections*, vol. VIII (1912), p. 158, and Isaac N. Arnold, *The Life of Benedict Arnold* (1880), p. 211.

57. Frothingham, *op. cit.*, passim.

58. *Writings of Washington*, vol. VIII, p. 198.

59. *Ibid.*, vol. XVIII, pp. 162, 166.

60. *Ibid.*, vol. IV, pp. 44, 57, 355, etc.

61. *Ibid.*, vol. IV, pp. 94, 119, 489; *ibid.*, vol. VII, p. 99, and vol. IX, pp. 211, 310.

62. *Ibid.*, vol. VIII, pp. 213-214, etc.

63. Josiah Quincy (editor), *The Journals of Major Samuel Shaw* (1847), p. 29; Worthington C. Ford (editor), *Correspondence and Journals of Samuel Blachley Webb* (3 vols., 1893-1894), vol. III, p. 327.

64. Kapp, *Life of Kalb*, p. 177.

65. Greene, *op. cit.*, vol. I, p. 101; *The Revolutionary War Letters of Captain Roger Welles of Wethersfield and Newington, Connecticut* (1932), pp. 18, 22.

66. Simms, *op. cit.*, p. 202; Frothingham, *op. cit.*, p. 240.

# Index

# INDEX

# INDEX